FINDHORN
Flower Essences

Dedication

* * * * * * * * * * *

This book is dedicated to the Angel of Findhorn

FINDHORN
Flower Essences

Straight to the Heart
of the Matter
· · · · · · · · · · · ·

Marion Leigh

FINDHORN
Press

Copyright © 1997 Marion Leigh
First published 1997
Reprinted 1998

ISBN: 1 899171 96 7

British Library Cataloguing-in-Publication Data.
A catalogue record for this book is available
from the British Library.

Book layout and cover design by David Gregson
Illustrations by Caragh McAuley

Printed by Interprint Ltd., Malta

Published in the UK by
Findhorn Press
The Park, Findhorn, Forres IV36 0TZ, Scotland
Tel. +44 (0)1309 690582 / Fax. 690036
email thierry@findhorn.org
http://www.findhorn.org/findhornpress/

Acknowledgements

My love and thanks to all the beings, seen and unseen, who have contributed to this work. I would like to acknowledge and thank in particular:

Dorothy Maclean, for the Foreword, and for her pioneering spirit.

Caragh McAuley, for her sensitive flower illustrations.

Judy Light, for her wisdom, practical assistance and attunement to the essences.

Jeremy Slocombe, for his help with editing, and for his faith in me over the years.

David Steel, for his nourishing love and care.

My children, Iona and Michael, for their patience, love and joyful presences.

My mother, Alice, for being the embodiment of love.

Disclaimer
· · · · · · · · · · ·

This book is for reference purposes only and is not in any way intended or claiming to be a substitute for properly qualified and licensed medical, psychological or other healthcare advice, diagnosis, treatment or prescription. Those who use flower essences do so by their own choice; and while if prepared and taken according to the instructions in this book, flower essences may prove efficacious, neither the author nor publisher promise, guarantee or accept responsibility for any specific result.

CONTENTS

Sources of quotes

Esoteric Healing by Alice A. Bailey, Lucis Press Ltd., London, 1953

Flowers and their Messages by The Mother, Sri Aurobindo Ashram Trust, India, 1973

Nature Spirits by Rudolf Steiner. Rudolf Steiner Press, London, 1995

Man's Supersensory and Spiritual Powers by G. Hodson, Theosophical Publishing House, India, 1977

Attunement by David Spangler, Findhorn Press (out of print) – From a study paper entitled *Attunement* which later appeared in *Anthology*

(All quotes reproduced by kind permission of the respective publishers)

FOREWORD

ALL OF NATURE is a doorway to the divine, and the beauty of flowers – their colours, their scents, their shapes, even their feel – continually amaze us, delight our senses and open our hearts. Somehow they speak to us on all levels, and reach into our essence.

Each one of us reacts differently to flowers. Nowadays people all over the world are recognising that flowers can not only delight us, but touch us deeply enough to change us. Perhaps change is the wrong word, for what they do as we open ourselves to their beauty is to awaken in us the same qualities that they embody. Their beauty is obvious, ours is often hidden. At this time, methods for making their essence available to us in a material form have been discovered.

Marion Leigh is one who is very open to the essence of flowers. Here she tells of her experience in connecting deeply with nature and how she was guided to make flower essences. Her story is naturally unique, for we are all unique beings. She shares how her story unfolds and how she was guided to continue to explore nature according to her own inner nature. As in all stories that tell of the wonderful world of nature, which is always talking to us if we would just listen, we are helped to connect with and recognise our own participation in the environment, in the world and we are helped to trust the workings of the universe. Stories of inner attunement confirm our links with all life, and above all, can help us to live our everyday life in the best way we know. The deeper our connections with everything around us, the more we appreciate life and its joys.

The quality most necessary for deep contact with anything is love. As we explore life, as we explore flowers, as we accept varying circumstances, as we grow, we realise more and more the power of love. So our love grows, and we become our own essence, which is love. Flower essences cannot but help us to this realization.

— *Dorothy Maclean*

INTRODUCTION

'Be like the flower. Radiate your beauty, your colour, your perfume. Be truly who you are. Open like the flower to the sun who gives you life.'

— from a Deva message

WE ALL LOVE FLOWERS. They have been a source of delight and happiness throughout time: their form, beauty, colour and perfume awaken all the senses and we immediately feel a sense of joy and wellbeing in their presence. Healing with flowers is among the most ancient of healing modalities. It is no surprise, therefore, that now the healing power of flowers is being rediscovered all over the world.

The subtle healing properties of flower essences restore equilibrium on all levels of being: physical, emotional, mental and spiritual. They can enhance personal development and are a powerful aid to transformation. They offer us the opportunity to address outworn behaviour patterns and negative states of mind which may contribute to or cause disease, emotional imbalance and spiritual disharmony. By stimulating the body's inherent ability to heal itself, flower essences restore order from a higher level and help to strengthen desirable or positive qualities such as courage, inner peace, love and acceptance.

Flowers contain the highest concentration of the life force of a plant. By the method of sun infusion, this life force is transferred into the water, charging it with the etheric or vibrational healing imprint of the flowers.

From the standpoint of vibrational medicine, the human being is viewed as being multidimensional, consisting of body, mind, and spirit. Linking the physical body with the subtle bodies of spirit is an energy network which feeds life force into the body and mind. Flower essences work by influencing the subtle energy bodies and systems, transforming the energy flow and thereby affecting the energetic patterns which influence life and consciousness. (Please see Energy Medicine and the Subtle Energy System.)

As with homoeopathic remedies, we do not know how flower essences actually work. However, scientific evidence of the existence of subtle energy systems is growing. Many flower essence producers are researching the efficacy of remedies, and ways of measuring effects are being undertaken using such methods as electro-scanning, Kirlian photography and Vegatesting.

The modern development of flower essence therapy is attributed to Dr Edward Bach, a respected Harley Street doctor, homoeopathic practitioner and sensitive, who experienced emotional and physical symptoms when he was near a particular flower. He discovered that by taking an essence of the flower, the symptoms were alleviated and that the same flower essence would heal similar emotional patterns in his patients. Bach was among the first to see the link between emotions, stress and illness.

Before Dr Bach, it is recorded that in the 1500s the great mystic healer Paracelsus collected the dew from flowering plants to treat his patients' emotional imbalances.

In the mid-1970s, nearly half a century after Bach left his legacy of the Bach Flower Remedies, new flower essences appeared. The Flower Essence Society in California began researching new essences, and in the 1980s and 1990s others were inspired, bringing us essences from around the world: from Australia, New Zealand, North and South America, South Africa, India and the Himalayas and Europe.

The pace of change in the world today, and the stresses and demands on humanity and on the environment can be disturbing and unsettling. All the new essences have come at a time when they are most needed, for healing and for transformation.

The elements of earth, air, fire and water combine to create the physical form of every plant according to the divine blueprint. The Findhorn Flower Essences have been created in cooperation with the forces of Nature. They are made using wild flowers from Scotland, and pure water collected from sacred healing wells. Our love and thanks must go to the angels, the divine architects; and to the nature spirits, who work according to The Plan to bring each plant into being. *Vis Mediatrix Naturae*, the healing power of Nature, is their gift to us in the form of flower essences. Through the love with which the essences are prepared, and the intention that those taking them maintain, these natural essences reaffirm our connection with the divine and the oneness of all life.

CO-CREATING THE ESSENCES

How does one give a precise meaning to a flower? The consciousness of the flower or plant is not a mental one. It is neither a sensation nor a feeling, but something of both, a spontaneous movement and vibration. If you are in contact with it, if you feel it, you can get an impression which may be translated as a thought. There is a kind of identification with the vibration, a perception of the quality that it represents. When there is this attunement, at the heart and through the feeling of love, you have a direct perception of what the plant may signify. The best way of opening to the deep influence of flowers is to love them.

—The Mother

MY FIRST DIRECT CONTACT with the nature intelligences began in Australia. I had taken a flower essence of Shooting Star, with the purpose of vivifying my inner and cosmic connections. I found myself waking at 3 a.m. every morning and during those hours began to receive inner messages in meditation. One message I received spoke of a connection with Antarctica, and of the potentiality of making Antarctic essences. It said that the time had come for the preparation of essences from Antarctica because of the comparative purity of that region. The essence of mosses and lichens, I was told, represents the primeval and primordial forces of Nature and would allow communication with the nature kingdoms through our deepest instincts and oneness. When very soon after that I told a colleague about the message, it turned out she was going to Antarctica! I asked her if she would be willing to make up the essence of mosses and lichens on my behalf and told her how to do it. (She later went on to develop essences from Antarctica herself.)

When my family and I came back to live at Findhorn in spring 1992, the entire area was vibrant with gorse in full bloom and I was drawn to preparing its essence. I decided to use water which I had collected from a little-known and very secluded, ancient local well with known healing properties (Braemou at Hopeman). This water, I was told, is a healing gift from the elemental kingdom of Nature; combined with the flowers, which embody the highest divine qualities of a plant, and in interaction with the human heart (of those preparing and using the essences) a powerful energy of transformation and healing is released.

One week later I was meditating in the Nature Sanctuary in the Findhorn Foundation when, unexpectedly, a being I identified as the Landscape Angel spoke to me of the overall thrust of the work that lay before me. It said that while many people tune into the angelic realms, few are able to communicate their wish for unification:

Angels and humans walk the path together. Hand in hand we help each other to reach God. But man is as yet unwilling to take his place beside us and we need willing co-workers who will bring our energies to bear force in the world... The landscape temple is alive with beings working consciously and creatively to make their presences felt. Those who can attune to us will be welcomed, embraced and guided to give our message to humankind. Give yourself in this work and together we will achieve unity, peace and healing of our earth.

At the time I was unsure of what this meant but felt encouraged to press on.

Making the flower essences led me into a very deep connection with Nature and the intelligences informing the nature kingdom—the devas or angels and the nature spirits of the elements. Sitting in meditation before a flowering plant, I would ask for guidance as to the qualities expressed by that plant, and which properties would be of healing benefit for humanity.

I continued to make flower essences but it was not until I did a workshop given by Dorothy Maclean at the Findhorn Foundation six months later that I found the confidence to speak out about it. For three magical days of the workshop, we participants were ushered into the angelic realms of mineral, plant, animal and superhuman realities. Dorothy explained how any sense of limitation restricted our contact, and asked us to examine what was holding us back. I received:

> *Success is dependent only upon your ability to consciously connect with us in spirit, in love and in the light. Will it to be so, and you are there, in oneness with life, with Nature and the realms of celestial beings who share the oneness in joy and with a spirit of surrender.*

Dorothy Maclean is pure inspiration. The workshop turned out to be a turning point for me. I no longer felt shy of speaking about my communications with the Nature intelligences and a few months later 'released' the first twelve flower essences I had prepared that year.

Each essence preparation has been an adventure in itself. During the time I begin to prepare an essence until the time I return to collect it, and following its final preparation, I experience its nature within myself, with the associated feelings and effects on all parts of my being. Also during the preparation time I almost always meet a person or persons who are personifications of the qualities expressed by the essence, or who may need it. It is this first-hand experience within myself — along with information received from the higher levels (and translated by my mind) and the message received from the over-lighting intelligences— that gives me a picture of the qualities of a flower. This is then an ongoing process of attunement, followed by research on the essences in a variety of therapeutic settings over extended periods of time by clients, friends and health practitioners, to study the indications, qualities and effects.

I had no overall plan to include any particular flowers in the range, and allowed myself to be guided in the moment, so that in a sense the flowers found me rather than me looking for them. The exception to this was the Scottish primrose, which I was strongly drawn to prepare. It is a rare plant, found only in certain areas on the north coast of Scotland and in Orkney. In the 1930s it had been sighted near Lossiemouth, ten miles away from Findhorn, but now it was nowhere to be found, despite my pestering friends and strangers alike to see if they had seen any. I finally discovered my Scottish primrose in a much-loved and cared-for garden on the Black Isle, and when I tuned in, the message that came through was so powerful in its implications that I knew why I had searched so thoroughly for it:

Amidst the wildness, the peace and serenity of this great free land, I grow in joy and wonder for the love of the land and the earth. The gift I bring is peace — peace in the heart of man. This I give in full comprehension of the reality of war and strife, and yet my time has come and I give myself joyfully in the knowing of God's grace for peace on earth, when man can embrace his brother in love and understanding, in forgiveness and compassion. Just one drop of my essence has the power to infuse the hearts of the masses, so treat me with great respect and I will manifest peace in God's graceful timing. Peace I bring when there is despair. Deliver me to the people of the world and my presence will permeate for all to realise the ultimate goal which is what I am: Peace on earth. I bring you glad tidings and leave you to reflect upon the import of my message. Praise Be to God on high and to all his ministers and agents of peace and goodwill. Blessings to all in the name of love and peace.

A remedy which is often indicated during the cold winter months here in the north of Scotland is Snowdrop. This essence was made by a workshop group in February when the land was still frozen; snowdrops are the first flowers to break through, having great strength and tenacity. We made the essence in the original garden of Findhorn two days after Findhorn Community co-founder Peter Caddy's sudden death. Here where he planted the first garden, we became aware of Peter's presence as we silently collected the snowdrops. We placed the bowl in the centre of the garden and attuned when the sun came out. Miraculously, the sun continued to shine until we returned to collect the essence many hours later. At this time of year in the far north sunshine is rare and unpredictable. I have found that when making an essence small miracles like this happen. I always ask for the support of the elemental beings in making an essence. When decanting the mother essence, I received:

Rejoice, rejoice, rejoice for I have come to herald the birth of the new. Cast away the old and embrace the destruction of the old decaying forms which no longer serve. I am the new, resurrected out of the embers of that fiery love which is what I am. I have two faces, one so horrible you would not know me there as God, and one so profound you cannot conceive it or believe it. I am the immortal fiery essence of God, instilled in the heart of man, of animal, of plant, of all that lives and breathes and moves and thinks itself into being. I am life. I am death. I am the fiery breath of God which creates and destroys by the Divine Will. I separate and divide, I bind and I loosen and I coalesce the energies of the substance which is the kernel of immortal life. I am the eternal flame.

Snowdrop speaks of our hopes and dreams for a life everlasting. Leaving behind the frozen darkness of winter, it is the joy of breaking new ground, of bursting through into the light and warmth of the sun. Making this essence during Peter's time of passing into the Light was no coincidence.

Making Snowdrop essence was the completion of making the first set of essences and also the beginning of the second, the Snowdrop being the first flower to appear after the long cold winter. When the next round of essences came into being, I noticed that many of them related to the first set but seemed to be on a higher spiral. For example, Snowdrop, with the keynotes of surrender and immortality, was another level of Stonecrop, which is for transition and transformation; and Laurel, for resourcefulness and manifestation was another turn of the spiral from Harebell, which is for prosperity and faith. With the third set of essences, this happened again, and joining Stonecrop and Snowdrop on another turn of the spiral came the essence of Hazel, whose keynotes are liberation and freedom. In the third spiral, Harebell and Laurel were succeeded by Sea Rocket.

I made up the essence of Sea Rocket on the White Strand of the Monks on Iona. I was sitting on the beach during the time of solarisation when a large moth with exquisitely beautiful markings landed before me. It seemed unable to lift itself up to fly and in its struggle, covered itself with sand. I carefully lifted the moth out of the sand and took it back to the house, placing it on the leaf of a plant. I returned a few hours later to see how the moth was doing and was surprised to see it had laid numerous eggs on the leaf.

When I sat in meditation to attune to the essence of Sea Rocket, I received:

Like the moth, I persevere against all resistance to reach my destination. Why do you find me here? Do you wonder at my succulence?

The message went on to say that despite the apparent destitution of the environment, the abundance of Nature is always present, that the power to exist and to manifest is within us, and within all life:

I cherish all that is given and with frugality transform the smallest seed into abundant blessings of life.

I'd like to share a few more stories on making the essences, to further illustrate how the nature of an essence is revealed.

✦ BALSAM ✦

During the time of making up the Balsam essence I took a walk to the beach at Findhorn. I ran along the beach and then walked into the icy cold sea. It felt delicious. I lunged in. Such energy, so invigorating! I went up into the dunes and found myself a little hollow out of the wind and lay in the sun, a powerful feeling of gratitude rising in my heart. As I lay there I prayed for healing and understanding. A few months earlier I had broken two fingers and they were still swollen and sore and the healing was slow. I took out my journal and wrote:

There's a man nearby in the dunes. He is standing up and is naked, exposing himself. I ignore him and turn my back. Spontaneously, I curl into the foetal position and place my broken fingers into my mouth. It feels strange to put them into my mouth as they are difficult to bend and the middle one is swollen and sore. In a dreamlike state, I become aware of being a foetus in my mother's womb, sucking these two fingers (the same two fingers I sucked as a child until I was seven years of age). Within the womb I feel peaceful, nurtured, complete. In the next moment I feel fear: I fear birth and separation from my mother. I hear myself say, 'I don't want to be alone', followed by the thought 'but I am already alone in here. And I am one with my mother.' With a rush I am back in the world of reality. Now the naked man has his gaze fixed on me. I must move on.

I returned to the garden to collect the essence, and when I attuned to it, I found it is for fostering feelings of trust, love, warmth, and nurturing. It helps us love and accept life, and the human physical bodies we have incarnated into as souls.

✢ Rose Alba ✢

Around the time of making the Rose Alba essence I had my first contact with the nature god, Pan. Sitting peacefully in the original garden, by the wild garden, I felt a strong presence. It was so close, I felt I could sense its breath. I felt unnerved, almost panicky and, afraid to open my eyes, said, 'you are too close'. I heard the crunching of pebbles on the path; someone was walking away. Prising open my eyes, I gazed around the garden. Every leaf, every plant, every flower was glowing with electric vibrancy and colour — I knew my inner vision was open. I became aware of two eyes glowing through the leaves in one of the trees. Like the images we see of the green man appearing through the foliage, he began to emerge from out of the tree. It was Pan, twelve feet tall, showing himself in his full glory. I sat in awe, no longer afraid. I heard him to say, 'I cast my seed forth into the Cosmic Mother's Womb.'

It was the height of summer and indeed seeds, like thistle down, seemed to be floating up to heaven as an offering. I have met Pan since then and he has shown himself to me in other forms, as the cloven-hooved, pipe-playing, dancing fawn; and as Lord of the Underworld of form, I understood the misrepresentation of him as the devil.

✣ Sycamore ✣

After collecting the Sycamore essence I trudged home completely exhausted. Falling onto the bed, I fell asleep, still wearing my coat and shoes! That evening there was a special dinner in the community centre for Sir George Trevelyan. He was making his last visit before passing into the Light. Now so frail that he could barely stand, Sir George rose to the occasion and gave a moving speech, the strength of his spirit shining through his worn-out physical body.

I had learned that day that the essence of Sycamore enables us to tap into the unlimited energy source of our inner light and life force, bringing strength and patience, and restoring gentleness and smoothness to our energy flow.

✣ The Air Element: Well of the North Wind ✣

After making this elemental essence on Iona, I returned to the nearby island of Erraid where I was staying, and went to meditate in the sanctuary, which overlooks Iona. I had received a message from the spirits of air when collecting the essence, so I did not expect another communication. I was amused when I heard: *'You humans are like the peacocks, strutting your egos. Strive to be more like the swan!'* This essence is about being free, like the sylphs, to soar to the heights of inspiration.

When I attune to the nature intelligence of a plant, I receive a message which speaks of the positive and highest attributes of an essence. In the case of Gorse, the quality I connected with was JOY. Accessing joy and light from within the self profoundly affects us on all levels and, in the case of Gorse, it is energising and promotes enthusiasm and stimulates immunity (through the spleen centre, which assimilates pranic energy, and the thymus).

I see a flower essence as being like a multifaceted diamond. I believe there are many facets to each flower essence and it is up to us to attune to these, to polish the diamond, so that the beauty of each facet is revealed. Only a relatively small amount of information, data and research is available about the many flower essences coming from all over the world and how they work. In time, when more research has been done, we will be able to see the whole picture of each remedy. This is why, with the Findhorn Flower Essences, it takes at least one year before I will release an essence for public use. Even though the information I initially receive from the nature intelligences makes it quite clear what the quintessence of each remedy is, for me it is a deep and therefore lengthy process to define an essence and its action on all the different levels of being: physical, emotional, mental and spiritual.

This aside, the landscape environment and its energies, the consciousness of the one making the essence, and the time (of day, of year) all affect the qualities of the remedy. For example, it is preferable to make up an essence whose effect and action is one of 'releasing', in the afternoon when the sunlight is decreasing in strength. Likewise, energies available at the time of the full moon are unique and can be used to enhance certain qualities of an essence.

So when the remedy of Gorse is made up in different landscapes, at different times, using different waters, it, and its effects, can be subtly yet powerfully altered. If we were truly macrobiotic, taking essences made locally would be ideal. However, we are planetary beings. Certainly in most of the western world we eat food from all over the globe. So an essence from Australia will work just as well in Scotland as an essence from Scotland will in Australia. The difference I have noticed in my practice in using local essences with local people is that the essences work very much faster so that they need not be taken for as long as remedies from other places, and the healing comes more swiftly.

Environment and consciousness play a big part in the making of an essence. Flowers selected for essence preparation should be growing in a pure landscape, away from pollution of any kind. They must be at the peak of flowering and in prime condition. An exception to this was when I made the essence of Daisy. I had grave doubts about it because I used flowers growing on a busy common area in the village of Findhorn. One morning a team of council gardeners appeared with lawnmowers and without a thought I rushed down to ask them to wait until I had picked some of the flowers. They watched bemused as I silently attuned, asked for permission, gave thanks, and proceeded to pick daisies and float them in my glass bowl. My doubts about including this flower essence in the repertory arose because of its very public, roadside location, but it came to me that this was the very reason for including it. Sure enough, when I tuned in, what I received confirmed that the essence of Daisy would help those seeking calm amidst the storm and hustle and bustle of urban life.

In a sense, the Findhorn Flower Essences made themselves. The very special environment of the Findhorn community gardens has provided the perfect foundation for their coming into being. My role in their co-creation has been simply that of an instrument and a channel for Spirit. The essences, like the flowers, belong to the world.

*A*TTUNEMENT, ALIGNMENT AND AWARENESS

To attune to the flowers you must be in conscious contact with your own soul or divine presence. Through this attunement one can become aware of the oneness of consciousness, of love, behind and in the whole of creation and then through this you can enter into contact with flowers and know the expression of the divine in the flower, the underlying aspiration of the flowers for the divine. Love of flowers brings you into the experience of love within the self and when you are perceptive to the inner expression within and between you, perhaps through the beauty of flowers, it can lead to an awakening by Nature within you to the consciousness underlying the manifested form.

— The Mother

✦ Magical Garden ✦

THE MAGIC of the Findhorn garden is world renowned: the Findhorn Foundation began in the garden, and the community which has grown up around it has done so through cooperation and attunement with the kingdoms of Nature. It is the expression and manifestation of its founders and those who have been guided to follow in their footsteps — attunement to the Divine Spirit within us and within all Nature around us. This deep connection with Nature continues to nourish and inspire all who come here.

I first came to live in the Findhorn Foundation in 1976. Curiously, I didn't work in the garden then, my work was in communications and networking.

I lived in the community for five years, following a spiritual practice of 'turning within'. I returned to my homeland, Australia, where my two children, Iona and Michael were born. I also qualified as a homoeopath. It was during my final years of study that I began to wonder about the Australian plants and their healing potential, and then I found my teacher and employer, Ian White of Australian Bush Flower Essences. I had three happy years working for the Bush Essences company, and as a homoeopath before I unexpectedly received a call to return to Findhorn.

The development of the Findhorn Flower Essences has been an education in itself for me. Guided by the conviction of my inner connections, I surrendered in trust to this knowing. With new confidence and with practice, this contact has strengthened over the years since I first began making the essences. I delight in being able to pass on to others my own teaching and experience of the practical application of attunement, alignment and awareness. The ability to communicate and connect with the angels and the nature beings is innate. Our task is to make it conscious. When, in our hearts and minds, and in the spirit of love, we bridge the seeming separation between us and the unseen spiritual world , we find joyful oneness with Nature, and the power to co-create with it.

✢ Oneness ✢

The process or practice of attunement is so simple a child can do it without thinking! As David Spangler says:

> We begin with understanding the concept of oneness, that there is no real separation and that everything exists within a unified field of being. The revealed nature of the oneness of creation is unfolding for us a dramatic and natural technique for transcending our human level of consciousness and communicating directly with vaster dimensions of being. We call this technique attunement.
>
> To communicate with a level of Life apparently outside us, we simply discover and attune to its corresponding reality within us. We realise there is no separation, that essentially we are one with that level and we accept that oneness as the reality. With the

practice of attunement, we find ourselves in increasing communication with higher and vaster realms of Life, both vertically in terms of higher frequency consciousness and horizontally in terms of physical life that surrounds us as fellow human beings and the lives within Nature.

Attunement is communication through communion, through recognising the wealth of oneness that has always been there. Unlike old-style communication which is seen as a flow between two or more centres or people and thereby maintaining the concept of separation, in attunement there is no flow between, there is oneness with.

In times past humanity lived closer to the land and in rapport with the rhythms and cycles of Nature. Modern civilisation has forgotten or even lost this connection.

The recognition that the world is in a delicate state of balance, the search for more harmonious lifestyles and the growing awareness of the subtle worlds brings back the need for understanding of working in cooperation with the nature kingdoms.

Living in accordance with God's law and the laws of Nature begins with inner alignment and attunement. From this awareness the garden at Findhorn grew and flourished. It nourished the minds, bodies and spirits of the people drawn to it, and this conscious cooperation with Nature within and without was the first principle in working in these gardens.

Attunement is the condition of being in oneness with and manifesting awareness, of the presence of being, the living presence of God in every living moment. How does one practice this state of awareness?

I asked Eileen Caddy, co-founder of the Findhorn Foundation, to tell me her way. She said that it is to be consciously aware, to be in the state of heart and mind balance, to be cognisant of God and the 'God waves' which are always there, and to switch on to them. 'And how do you do that? I asked. 'Meditation, prayer, listening switches you on' was her reply. 'We have to bring it about by our awareness.'

So the first step is being still. Have you noticed times of being in Nature when you have been absorbed by the beauty all around you?. Watching an ant busy at work, hearing the sounds of Nature, wind rustling in the trees, the flowing river, brings a sense of peace to our being. Sometimes we don't even notice it because it is very subtle. In these moments we experience oneness with Nature. Then the mind wakes up once more and brings us back to 'everyday consciousness', and we forget, as if it had been a dream.

Eileen's methods enable us to attain this state of attunement. And like the child, we can harmonise the self with Nature through simple observation and stillness. When we identify with Nature, reflect and observe our relationship changes, separateness gives way. Dorothy Maclean says it is choosing to be in the superconscious. It is a case of *feeling into* Nature, of awakening the inner senses to inner perceptions. We move into a state of knowing or intuition beyond the concrete lower mind and into the world of feeling. To make this connection requires clear motivation or intention, trust in ourselves, and practice!

✢ Spirit of The Elements ✢

In my own practice of attunement I always acknowledge and praise the presences of the elemental nature spirits. These are the spirit beings of earth, air, fire and water who are the builders of form, the blueprint being held by the devas or angels, the architects of form.

Elemental energies fuel us with the fuel we need to feel alive. Each elemental being reflects a basic energy pattern as it builds and manifests in Nature. These interweave to create and sustain all matter on earth. It is said that in working with us the elemental beings are able to move higher within the hierarchy of life. Learning to work with them is a dynamic way of attuning to all of the energies of Nature and their effects upon us. It facilitates 'control' over our own energy systems on all levels.

My awareness of the elementals was heightened when I was drawn to making essences which embodied the elements. Sitting by the Findhorn River one sunny day in the summer of '93, I was mesmerised by the power of the flowing water and, without a second thought, took out my glass bowl to prepare an essence. I felt the power of the river, the channel for the lifeblood, feeding and nourishing this landscape. I also prepared essences encapsulating the qualities of earth, air, fire and ether. These essences share common key characteristics: oneness with Spirit, supreme power, limitless energy, freedom, mobility, indestructibility, eternal life, humour and transmutation and metamorphosis. I use the elemental essences in the environment: for healing, cleansing, celebration and ritual. (Please see Elemental Essence Messages).

The spirits of the earth are sometimes referred to as gnomes and they are the fosterers of life. As Rudolf Steiner says, they, with the help of the fire spirits 'instil life into the plant and push it upwards. They carry the life ether to the root, the same life ether in which they live. For gnomes the solid earth is hollow and offers no resistance. Gnomes transform the spirit currents flowing downward from the blossom and fruit into the roots and carry the ideas of the whole universe streaming throughout the world.'

Water spirits are also known as undines. Without water there would be no life, and the spirits of water bring replenishment. Our ancestors regarded water as a living creature with the power to bestow the life force, health and energy. The undines symbolise abundant energy. In humans they maintain the astral body, the flowing streams of the body and stimulate the feeling nature. Working with them can assist us in controlling and directing dream activity, and in feeling the fullest ecstasy of the creative acts of life. In the plant world, Rudolf Steiner says the undines work with the leaves. 'In their dreaming they bind and release in their weavings the substances of the air which they mysteriously introduce into the leaves. They are the world chemists.'

Air Spirits or sylphs bring inspiration and creativity. Many work for the creation of air and the atmospheric currents. In the human being they maintain the mental body, help stimulate new knowledge and inspiration and assist in using intuitive and rational thinking together. Through breath and air we assimilate power. The true power of the word is awakened with the aid of the spirits of air and they are critical to the development of clairaudience and telepathy. The energy is stimulating, changeable and can awaken greater intellect and strength of will. Steiner says the sylphs 'live in the air warmth element... press toward the light, relate themselves to it — to the vibrations in a body of air. This spiritually sounding, moving element of air. They absorb what the power of light sends into these vibrations of the air... the cosmic bearers of love through the atmosphere, the bearers of wishes of love through the universe.'

In the plant their 'task is to bear light into the plant. The power of the sylphs in the plant works on the chemical forces which were induced into the plant by the undines. Here occurs the interworking of sylph-light and undine chemistry. The sylphs weave out of the light the ideal plant form.'

The elementals of fire are called salamanders and bring stimulating, radiant vitality. Fire spirits, as agents of transmutation, transformation and regeneration, hold the keys to the processes of alchemy. The fiery element is both constructive and destructive, assisting in destroying the old and building the new and so very effective in healing work, helping to develop catalytic healing energies. Their energies are very stirring; their effect vitalising, and capable of stimulating strong emotional currents and passions, which are sometimes difficult to control and direct. For this reason, when working with these elementals, it is best to always maintain an attitude of tranquil, placid contentment; then they will instil great inspiration and spiritual idealism and perception. The fire spirits are enticed by music and strong rhythms.

In plants, Steiner says, 'they are the inhabitants of the warmth-light element. When warmth of earth is at its height or otherwise suitable, they gather the warmth together... carry it to the blossoms of the plants... carry the warmth into the seed... carry concentrated cosmic warmth on the little airships of anther-pollens.'

✢ The Shining Ones ✢

Guiding and directing the work of the elemental beings stand the angels, or devas. (The word 'deva' comes from the Sanskrit and means 'shining one'.)

People who are close to Nature, artistic and sensitive seem most able to contact the devic kingdom, particularly in parts of the world where there are mountains, seas, lakes, where there are beauty spots almost 'magical' in their atmosphere.

The idea that there are such beings is not a new one, and much of the world's literature down through the ages is replete with myths, legends, fairy-tales and allegories relating to the shining ones.

Throughout all time of which records exist, men have borne testimony to their perception of forces, phenomena and beings not normally visible. Despite wide separation both in time and space, there is a remarkable resemblance between the myths, the legends and particularly the descriptive folklore of the various peoples of the earth. This universality, similarity and persistence throughout the ages of belief in the Kingdom of the Angels is strong evidence, I submit, for the existence of a kernel of reality within that belief, a basis of fact upon which folklore is founded. *

My understanding of the deva-angel-human relationship is that we belong to a composite body and work together to fulfil the purposes of natural law and human evolution. From the smallest to the highest, each being has its own particular work to perform and as the most exalted angel uses its mighty intelligence in the forming of worlds, so the tiny nature spirit uses its powers in directing the processes of the plant kingdom. It is by coming into closer contact with Nature that we will become more and more at one with her spirit, and understand the depths of her beauty. The unfolding of conscious relating between the devic, angelic and human kingdoms will facilitate each learning from and helping the other; for all life, whether visible or invisible, is subject to one Spiritual Law, and each part must work together to carry out fully the Divine Will. In unfolding our collective purpose through conscious contact and communication with the devic or angelic realm, humanity may discover its true place in the scheme of things.

September Poem

By Michael Hedley Burton

Spirits of water, spirits of air
Weave through the world
Full of nurture and care
Sons of bright fire
Gnomes of quick gait
All of them speak to me
Whilst they create
Oh, we work within the world
For purest joyfulness alone
But remember please the deeds we do
They must not go unknown
For you free us from enchantment
When you make your life our own.

ENERGY MEDICINE AND THE SUBTLE BODIES

The soul is the healer within the form and true spiritual healing comes about through the evocation and downpouring of the soul's energy into the etheric vehicle sweeping it into a new condition of brilliance, thus conditioning directly the dense physical form.

— Alice Bailey

FLOWER ESSENCES have been described as 'liquid drops of consciousness'. They are energy medicine, and work on the etheric and subtle bodies, on the deep levels which affect the energetic patterns that influence life and consciousness. In order to see how flower essences work, it is helpful to know something of the subtle or etheric body, with the understanding that the human being is multidimensional, consisting of body, mind, soul and spirit.

The etheric body conditions, controls and determines the life expression of the individual. It is the conveyor of the forces of the personality and therefore galvanises the physical body into activity. As the chakras govern areas of the body and glands, healing energies may be effectively channelled through them, and balancing may be directly achieved with the aid of flower essences.

The etheric body underlies and permeates the physical body and contains the energetic blueprint of our physical structure. Any imbalances in this body are reflected in the condition of the other bodies: physical, emotional and mental and spiritual. In the etheric body there are seven major chakras, or energy centres, which provide points of connection for energy to flow from one subtle plane to another. The word 'chakra' literally means 'wheel'. The chakras take in, assimilate and process energy of higher vibrations. These energies are then blended and transformed to create the secondary energies needed to vitalise the whole being.

Chakras receive energies from a variety of sources — some cosmic (prana), some environmental, familial and ancestral, and some from the collective unconscious. The activity of the chakras is determined by the inner development of the individual, that is, the quality of their physical, emotional and spiritual being.

Incoming primary energy is received by the chakras, and then, according to chakra quality, it is there blended to create secondary energies, which flow outwards via the *nadis*, or chakra meridians, to affect the nervous and endocrine systems, as well as the blood. The bloodstream is the carrier of the Life Principle to all parts of the body. Free circulation of the life essence is paramount to good health and wellbeing.

The chakras are responsible for the correct functioning of the entire organism, producing both physiological and psychological effects. They govern the glands, which have a direct relation to the bloodstream, conditioning the major areas of the body. The four major agents of distribution of the life energies are the etheric body, the endocrine system, the nervous system and the bloodstream: four aspects of one vital circulatory system which work as one integrated whole.

Chakra Imbalances

Chakras are subject to over-stimulation, under-stimulation and blockage. This may express as areas of stress, overemphasis or denial of the personality. Or they may be affected by more objective factors, such as miasms (inherited and acquired deviations of the energy body which predispose one to patterns of chronic disease).

When chakras are blocked, this can manifest as disturbances in the physical, emotional or mental wellbeing, impeding the flow of life energies and hindering soul growth. Negative emotions, such as anxiety, suppress chakra activity. If chakras are over-stimulated, acute inflammations may occur in the physical body; if under-stimulated, more chronic problems may surface.

The following summary of the major chakras, their location and function will help those unfamiliar with these energy vortices to identify and understand the way some of the flower essences work in linking, opening, purifying and facilitating free flow of energies.

The Crown Chakra

This chakra is the distributing agent of the energy of Divine Will. The organ of synthesis, it relates spirit and personality. Located just above the top of the head, this chakra governs the upper brain and right eye. As the seat of the soul, it is said to represent the spiritual will-to-be, whilst processing external information and relating cosmic principles of truth to the other planes. It rules the pineal gland, which is electromagnetic and photosensitive, the seat of the 'third eye'. The pineal gland anchors the Consciousness Principle.

The Ajna Chakra/Third Eye

This centre is the distributing agent of the energy of Active Intelligence. Located at the point between the eyebrows, this chakra governs the lower brain, left eye, ears, nose and nervous system. Related to the throat centre, it links the spiritual triad (spirit, soul and intelligence) to the personality. As the seat of the integrated personality, it works towards individuation and the expression of idealism, imagination and desire.

The Throat Chakra

This chakra is the organ for distribution of creative energy, specifically of the creative WORD. It registers the intention or creative purpose of the soul, which is transmitted to it by the inflow of energy from the ajna centre or third eye. It governs the lungs, bronchial and vocal parts and the alimentary canal. Centre of the intelligence and the creative expression of thought and emotion, it is very active in many people. Located on the spine at the back of the neck, it rules the thyroid gland and to a lesser extent the parathyroid and parotid glands.

The Heart Chakra

The centre for registration and distribution of Divine Love poured out via the soul, this chakra governs the heart, circulatory system, blood and vagus nerve. It rules group interests and anchors the Life Principle. The gland it rules is the thymus, involved with hyper- and auto-immune reactions. Excess energies in the solar plexus may strain this chakra.

The Solar Plexus Chakra

This centre is the organ of desire, the instrument through which emotional energy flows and the outlet of the astral body into the outer world. As the recipient of all emotional reactions and of desire impulses and energies, this collection centre gathers in all the lower energies and is a focal point for direction and distribution of these collected energies, transferring them to the higher centres. Located just below the level of the shoulder blades on the spine, this chakra rules self-interest and the emotional life, as well as the regions of the pancreas, stomach, liver, gall bladder and nervous system.

The Sacral Chakra

Located at the base of the lumbar spine, level with the navel, the sacral chakra is the centre of the creative sexual energies and governs the reproductive system and the gonads. If found to be overactive, this centre may be balanced by visualising, in meditation, that excess energy is drawn up to the throat chakra, to be expressed there.

The Base Chakra

This centre feeds the life-giving principle, the will-to-live, to all parts of the body and expresses the energy of Spiritual Will. Located at the coccyx, at the base of the spine, it rules the physical will-to-be and the self-preservation instincts. It's associated adrenal glands help us to sense danger and cope with stress.

*W*ORKING WITH FLOWER ESSENCES

Earth's flowers spring up and laugh at Time and Death.

— Sri Aurobindo

How to Choose Flower Essences

CHOOSING A FLOWER ESSENCE by reading the descriptions of flower essences is not always easy. Often we can relate to so many of the essences we end up wanting to put them all into one bottle! Rarely do I mix more than four essences together, and then only if they are complementary, addressing related issues and symptoms. (For examples, please see Combination Essences on page 79.) Otherwise, I find it is very powerful to prescribe a single essence which, like a homoeopathic constitutional remedy, will have a deep-acting and lasting effect.

'Constitutional prescribing' is determining and matching a single remedy based on the personality type of the individual: this includes his or her temperament, qualities, behaviour and symptoms.

The basis for successful flower essence selection is to look for key emotional, psychological and soul issues, seeking understanding and awareness of present problems and challenges, as well as those of the past. Some areas to look at might include: childhood, emotions, energy levels, fear, life changes, mental clarity, motivation, environmental influences, physical health, relationships, self-esteem, sexuality, stress, sleep, shock, trauma, and thought patterns. Choosing essences for oneself requires honesty and self reflection.

Other methods of selection include using the intuition; muscle testing, or kinesiology, and dowsing with a pendulum. Even if you are confident in these methods objectivity is needed, and for best results a knowledge of the essences and the issues being addressed. When tuning in, read the descriptions and get a sense of which essences intuitively feel right. Then use one or other of the methods listed above to corroborate your choice.

Where there is a serious physical or psychological problem, it is crucial to seek professional help. An experienced practitioner will usually take a detailed case history including medical history and presenting physical symptoms (digestive problems, circulatory problems, sleeping, breathing difficulties and blood pressure problems); personality traits; lifestyle; stress levels at home and at work; relationships; mental, emotional and spiritual issues; mental symptoms; predominant feelings such as anger, grief, depression, sadness and fear; purpose, direction and motivation; self-esteem and so on. A practitioner can also give support and insight when the essences bring up painful feelings or confront us with difficult decisions.

How to Use Flower Essences

Flower essences are normally taken orally. Like homoeopathic remedies, they are absorbed through the mucus membranes in the mouth. I usually recommend taking seven drops under the tongue three times a day for about two weeks. With some essences, or combination of essences, a single dose may be all that is required. On the other hand, in the case of trauma or acute pain, a remedy such as *First Aid* can be taken every fifteen minutes until symptoms subside.

You can also use flower essences in other ways: topically, applied directly to the skin, or added to a good quality base cream; or in the bath by putting a few drops of stock essence in the bath water. They can also be dispersed into the air (for example, when cleansing a space) using an atomiser spray bottle or by evaporation in a clean aromatherapy burner.

Stock and Dose Dilutions

I almost always use or prescribe an essence in dose dilution. Apart from being more economical (a 15 ml stock bottle will make up about 30 dosage bottles), it follows the homoeopathic principle of the greater the dilution, the more effective the remedy.

To prepare a ready-to-take dosage bottle from stock concentrate, take a clean 25 ml bottle and fill three quarters with pure water and one quarter with brandy. To this add seven drops of stock essence.

How to Make Flower Essences

The favoured method of making flower essences is by sun infusion. Flowers contain the highest concentration of the life force of a plant, and the essence is an etheric or vibrational infusion in which water is charged with the flowers' life force. By the method of sun infusion, the vibrational imprint of the flowers is transferred into the water.

When making an essence it is important that the flowers be in prime condition and from plants which are not in any way polluted. Flowers are collected, preferably using a leaf, so that the fingers do not touch them, and floated in a glass bowl filled with pure water. The entire surface area of the bowl should be covered with flowers. The bowl is then placed in the sunshine for a number of hours (in Scotland it is about four). The pure essence is then decanted by separating the flowers and original tincture and mixed 50/50 with brandy as a preservative. This is the mother tincture which is then diluted a number of times to prepare a ready-to-take dosage bottle.

see next page ▶

Original Tincture

floral infusion

Mother Tincture

Stock Bottle

50% brandy alcohol to which is
added 50% original tincture
(floral infusion)

1/3 brandy alcohol + 2/3
pure water + 7 drops
Mother Tincture

Dose Bottle

1/4 brandy alcohol + 3/4 pure
water + 7 drops stock essence
(ready to take)

How to Store Flower Essences

To ensure the life of flower essences, store away from light, heat, perfumes,
chemicals and aromatics.

FLOWER ESSENCE REPERTORY

✣ Index ✣

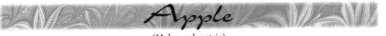

Apple

(Malus sylvestris)

✽ *Keynotes:* HIGHER PURPOSE and WILL-TO-GOOD

The essence of Apple helps us to integrate our desires and our willpower to realise positively our goals and visions. By aligning with Higher or Divine Purpose we channel these powerful energies into right action.

✽ *Attributes:*

Development and the right use of the will, removing blockages to positive action; concertedness; inner strength to overcome inertia; self-discipline; humility; obedience to higher will; reforming lower desire into love and selfish will into will-to-serve.

✽ *Indications:*

Blocks to realising inherent power and ability; inability to sustain self-discipline; the glamour of power and superiority; lack of the power to act or lack of self-assertion; succumbing to lower desires; unbalanced sexual expression; depletion of creative sexual forces.

Apple facilitates the contacting of our higher aspirations, freeing our attachment to our personal desires and enabling us to use our will to truly serve for the good of all.

Affirmation:

I align myself with my Higher Purpose and act for the good of all.

Balsam

(Impatiens glandulifera)

❀ *Keynotes:* RELATIONSHIP and INTIMACY

Balsam essence facilitates love and acceptance of the physical bodies we have chosen to incarnate into as souls. We feel fully present in the world and can express feelings of true love.

❀ *Attributes:*

Capacity for intimacy and expression of love; to nurturing and nourishing oneself and others; feeling at home in one's body and environment; awareness of bodily needs, sensations and feeling; warmth; sensitivity; sensuality; relationship bonding; celebrating sexuality; healing with the mother/feminine aspect; creative feminine power; connecting with mother Nature.

❀ *Indications:*

Fear of separation; life or birthing; fear of intimacy; feeling unloved or unwanted; feeling neglected; abandoned or rejected, feeling rootless or homeless; lack of bonding; alienation from the mother or the feminine aspect of self; fear of relationships; reduced physical warmth and presence; physical dislike; frigidity; aloofness; permissiveness; exhibitionism; unfulfilled desire.

When we feel out of place, ill at ease or fail to nourish ourselves, we may have difficulties relating and feel separated from others or unloved. Balsam reminds us of the divinity of our being in physical form. We experience feelings of warmth, sensitivity and tenderness towards ourselves and others, and a new joy and harmony in our relationships.

Affirmation
I am happy and at home in my body and in the world.

(Erica cinerea)

✿ *Keynotes:* STABILITY and SELF-CONFIDENCE

Bell Heather essence helps to access inner strength and the resolve to stand one's ground after stress, trauma or conflict.

✿ *Attributes:*

Tenacity; affirmation; trust in one's inner knowing; faith in oneself; standing up for oneself; being resolute in stance and purpose; assertiveness; following one's own path with confidence; resilience; self-recovery.

✿ *Indications:*

Loss of faith in oneself; lack of confidence; mood swings; being easily swayed; feeling victimised by circumstance; loss of direction or purpose; fragility.

Bell Heather is stabilising. It allows consolidation and the strength to stand firm while remaining flexible. After setback, disappointments or misfortune, essence of Bell Heather helps to foster trust and faith in the self.

Affirmation:

I stand firmly and securely in my being.
I have faith and trust in my self.

Birch

(Betula pendula)

❦ *Keynotes:* PERCEPTION and VISION

Birch essence helps us to broaden our perceptions and transcend limitations of mind. Through expanding our consciousness and seeing our cosmic connections we gain understanding and peace of mind.

❦ *Attributes:*

Bringing in the light of the mind; expanding one's awareness into the cosmos; contacting Universal Mind; direct experience of the infinite here and now; deep mindfulness; realising the inner wisdom of life experiences; cultivating spiritual vision; focused and intuitive attitude and the power to see the vision and direct one's course to it.

❦ *Indications:*

Obscured or unclear vision; being stuck in thought patterns which hold one back; inability to see beyond oneself and one's concerns; worry; introspection; dulled senses; living in the past or future; escapism or daydreaming; out-of-body states; 'blind spots'; not learning from past mistakes; confusion of mind.

Essence of Birch facilitates breakthrough to understanding the causes of our life circumstances and predicaments. When we identify with our lower self, conflicts or behaviour patterns, it can influence or restrict how we view ourselves and the world and thus impede our highest aspirations. Birch essence frees our imagination and gives us hope for the future.

Affirmation:

I open my mind to new ways and understanding.

(Cytisus scoparius)

❀ *Keynotes:* CLARITY and ILLUMINATION

Broom essence stimulates mental clarity and concentration, facilitating ease in communication and creative thought when in a state of bewilderment.

> ❀ *Attributes:*
> Mental clarity; concentration; communication; integration; decision making; self-expression; guidance; intuition; creative thought; clarity of purpose.
>
> ❀ *Indications:*
> Memory loss; dullness; feeble-mindedness; bewilderment; confusion; lack of integration; coordination or communication.

Broom brings light into our minds. When our mental body is clouded or dull or when we are distracted, we are hindered in our expression and communication. Essence of Broom allows the light of the intuition to illuminate our minds, inspiring us with its brilliance and bringing creative thought into outer expression.

Affirmation:
*My mind is clear.
I express myself, my thoughts and
ideas with ease.*

Daisy

Common Daisy (Bellis perennis)

❀ *Keynotes:* INNOCENCE and GRACE

Essence of Daisy allows us to remain calm and centred amid turbulent surroundings or overwhelming situations, creating a safe space in which to be vulnerable.

> ❀ *Attributes:*
>
> Calmness and centredness amid intense activity; lightness; presence; being or staying on purpose; protection; ability to enjoy; rediscovery of innocence; playfulness.
>
> ❀ *Indications:*
>
> Being overwhelmed; fear of losing control; distraction; confusion; being easily swayed; inconsistency; indifference; being 'up in the clouds'; fickleness; over-sensitiveness.

Daisy helps us to maintain innocence, vulnerability and sensitivity when in our busy lives we fear losing our calm centre within the storm. The essence of Daisy helps us to stay on purpose and on course, and protects us while we do so.

Affirmation:

I am calm and centred and feel safe in my world.

(Sambucus nigra)

❀ *Keynotes:* BEAUTY and REJUVENATION
Essence of Elder stimulates the body's natural powers of recuperation and renewal. It helps us to contact and radiate the beauty and joy of our inner eternal youth.

> ❀ *Attributes:*
> Invoking recuperative powers of the body; self-acceptance; enthusiasm; youthfulness; acknowledgement of the process of ageing; lightening-up; new energisation on cellular level through increased inflow of *pranic* energy; revealing and radiating one's true being and beauty; joyful expression of the physical body.

> ❀ *Indications:*
> Feeling unworthy or self-conscious; dislike of oneself or one's body; feeling ugly, heavy or old; overidentification with one's image; dullness; subdued or held-in personality; masking of the True Self; lack of personal vitality or aliveness.

Through Essence of Elder we allow greater penetration into our bodies of the sun forces which regenerate us. Our energy centres or chakras become irradiated, bringing feelings of well-being and thus illuminating our inner beauty.

Affirmation:
*I am renewed and revitalised.
I radiate the beauty and joy of
my wellbeing.*

Globe-Thistle

(Echinops sphaerocephalus)

❦ *Keynotes:* AT-ONE-MENT and WHOLENESS

Globe-Thistle essence helps us recognise the order of life and our evolutionary process, enabling us to willingly and joyfully make sacrifices which will liberate us on our path.

❦ *Attributes:*

Wholeness through balance; centredness; temperance; giving oneself in service to humanity and to the world; self-sacrifice; radiating strength and flexibility; goodwill; Christ/sun/cosmic wholeness; peace and humility; stable; supportive energy; ability to accept the suffering of others; empathy; patience; willingness to moderate; sobriety; restitution.

❦ *Indications:*

Personal handicap; misfortune or discouragement; preoccupation with personal suffering or loss; feeling a victim; martyrdom; self-condemnation; feeling chained to the wheel of life; addictions; self-indulgence; self-gratification; self-pity; waspishness; irritability.

Often we hold on to the non-essential aspects of our lives rather than risk the pain of letting go. With Globe-Thistle we reconnect with the inner strength and the flexibility to free ourselves from burden. We discover that surrendering to a higher order for the good of the whole brings us the deepest peace and joy.

Affirmation:
I am strong and whole.
I serve joyfully in the spirit of goodwill.

Gorse

(Ulex europaeus)

❀ *Keynotes:* JOY and PASSION FOR LIFE

Essence of Gorse is a light bringer, stimulating vitality, enthusiasm and motivation at times of apathy and low immunity, bringing light-heartedness and enjoyment of life.

> ❀ *Attributes:*
>
> Renewal of life force; vitality; motivation; enthusiasm; living in the moment; enjoyment and celebration of life.
>
> ❀ *Indications:*
>
> Apathy; burn out; low immunity; listlessness; lack of motivation or joy; inability to join in or to share oneself.

Gorse is a bringer of light, heralding joy — that soul quality which can heal us. When we run ourselves down, we have no energy left to participate fully in life. We risk withholding our energies in order to conserve them for ourselves but in so doing deny ourselves the very source of replenishment we require. Essence of Gorse brings us back to the enjoyment of living every moment to the full. It gives us hope. This strengthens the will and the body's immunity.

Affirmation:
I live my life with joy and passion.

Grass of Parnassus

(Parnassia palustris)

❀ *Keynotes:* TRANSLUCENCY and SERENITY

Essence of Grass of Parnassus transforms and diffuses the powerful inflowing universal energies into a gentle and graceful vibration which uplifts our souls and opens the heart to the healing power of love.

❀ *Attributes:*

Inner peace and spiritual receptivity; emptying the chalice of one's being to inflow from the spiritual source; power of vulnerability; radiating the pure light of love; purity of heart; transmuting power into love; feminine receptive qualities: gentleness, softness, delicacy, subtlety; openness and gracefulness; modesty; innocence; virtuousness; releasing sadness and sorrow.

❀ *Indications:*

Conflicts between power and love; fear of being in one's power; faint-heartedness; delicacy; protective barriers to feeling deep pain and strong emotion; hardening oneself to pain; deep sadness and sorrow; fear of helplessness or vulnerability; guarding oneself with shields of self-protection; feeling 'out of control'; holding back in sharing oneself; elusiveness; coyness.

When we feel weighed down by strong emotions, fear or vulnerability, we may create protective barriers which cut us off from our true feelings. Grass of Parnassus opens us to full expression of the Self and to access soul qualities of bliss, peace, joy and serenity.

Affirmation:
I open my heart to let in love.
I feel and express my love in the world.

Harebell

Scottish Bluebell (Campanula rotundifolia)

❀ *Keynotes:* PROSPERITY and FAITH

Harebell essence is for realigning to the spirit of abundance and releasing material concerns caused by fear of lack.

❀ *Attributes:*

Manifesting abundance; re-alignment; affirmation; balance; self-reliance; equilibrium.

❀ *Indications:*

Fear of lack; possessiveness; lack of faith; attachment; poverty consciousness; feeling out of alignment with oneself and one's environment.

Harebell is about realigning with Spirit. When we lose faith in ourselves, we may block the flow of spiritual energies. Fear of lack can produce attachment and possessiveness, hindering our ability to give and receive. Essence of Harebell opens our awareness to all that life has to offer and allows us the grace and gratitude to accept it.

Affirmation:

I align myself with the spirit of abundance and have faith that all my needs are met.

Hazel

(Corylus avellana)

❀ *Keynotes:* LIBERATION and FREEDOM

Hazel essence can help free us to flow with the river of life. Letting go of all that restricts one's growth, advancement and potential unfoldment, we discover the joy and bliss of surrendering as we travel into the unknown.

❀ *Attributes:*

Flowing with and trusting the Source; acceptance and trust in the progression of one's life path and destiny; unfoldment and realisation of one's purpose and potential; perseverance in attaining one's goals and objectives; motivation to carry through; intentionality; catalyst to stimulate movement and freedom of action; faith to overcome obstacles; joyful liberation and surrender.

❀ *Indications:*

Failure to meet one's goals and objectives; lack of power to follow through; procrastination; over-controlling the flow and direction of one's life; fear or inability to break free of old ties; attachments to the past; keeping within self-imposed limits; fear of failure or making mistakes; not daring to move out of one's depth; discouragement; disappointment; dissatisfaction; frustration; agitation; restlessness without direction.

We often use considerable effort and energy trying to control the direction and flow of our lives, by hanging on to what has ceased to serve us, or through the limitations of our thinking. Hazel essence brings us present in time, helping us to shatter the bonds which bind us to the past . We move forward in the wonder and joy of newness and trust the power of the infinite movement as we let life flow freely.

Affirmation
I travel forward in life with
wonder and joy.

(Crataegus sp.)

❀ *Keynotes:* REBIRTH and CREATION

Holy-Thorn essence opens our hearts to the love and the acceptance of ourselves and others, allowing intimacy and the expression of our truth and creativity.

> ❀ *Attributes:*
> Birthing and expressing creative activity on all levels; opening to others; intimacy and nurturing; radiant compassion; warm and loving acceptance of all; universal Christ-like love; transformation through the power of love.

> ❀ *Indications:*
> Blocked self-expression and creativity; withholding oneself; lack of involvement; creating barriers to friendship; fear of rejection; repression of the True Self.

Holy-Thorn essence is made from the flowers of the Glastonbury Thorn. The original tree is said to have grown from the stave of Joseph of Arimathea where he struck it on Wearyall Hill in Glastonbury. This essence awakens us to the presence of the love of the Christ in ourselves and others.

Affirmation:

I open my heart to feel and express love and acceptance of myself and others.

Iona Pennywort

Wall Pennywort
(Umbilicus rupestris)

❀ *Keynotes:* PERSPICACITY and TRANSPARENCY

Essence of Iona Pennywort brings light into the darkest corners of our souls. Through conscious recognition of the shadow self, we can let go of unfounded fears, understanding that the darkness serves to highlight the essential truth of our being.

❀ *Attributes:*

Bringing in the light of conscious awareness; facing the truth when it comes to light; mastering the forms of darkness in the underworld; acknowledging and integrating all aspects of the self; confronting hidden fears honestly; the quest for the Truth; the spirit of renewal; the protective Light of the Holy Spirit; obedience to the Laws of Spirit; trial of strength; discipline; observance; making amends; redemption; salvation; impeccability; being without judgement.

❀ *Indications:*

Glamour of the Path of Light; denial of the shadow side; concealing the darkness within; fear of the dark; nightmares; hiding one's dark thoughts; negativity; dark or demonic thoughts or states of mind; psychic fears: possession, supernatural or demonic forces, superstition, fascination with the powers of darkness; secrecy; distorting or veiling the truth from oneself or others; suspicion; delusion; torment; paranoia; temptation; pride; transgression or defiance of spiritual laws; judgement; guilt; remorse; shame.

When we deny or fear the dark aspects of ourselves, or of life, we create illusion and self-deception, and judgement of ourselves and others. With Iona Pennywort we realise that the darkness co-exists as part of the whole to reveal the clarity and brilliance of the Light. We move forward with a new awareness and purity of aspiration.

Affirmation:
*I acknowledge and respect all aspects of myself.
I am light.*

(Alchemilla vulgaris)

❀ *Keynote:* AWARENESS and OMNISCIENCE

Lady's-Mantle essence allows us to access the infinite knowledge and wisdom available to us through the unconscious mind. From this union of unconscious and conscious knowing we realise deeper awareness.

❀ *Attributes:*

Bringing the light of consciousness into the unconscious; embracing all-knowing unlimited wisdom; integrating soul life with ordinary reality; surrender to and trust in the inner knowing of the True Self; receptivity to spiritual wisdom through dreams and the realm of archetypes; interpreting symbols from the unconscious; coordination of rational and abstract thinking; comprehension; responsiveness; powers of observation; mindfulness; communication.

❀ *Indications:*

Limiting one's understanding to the conscious, rational mind; lack of imagination or vision; insensibility to the inner world of feeling; short attention span; being easily distracted; ignorance; apathy; dyslexic disorders; unthinkingness; unmindfulness; daydreaming; impassivity; non-responsiveness; guardedness; conservatism; scepticism; overreaction; projecting out one's problems.

When we are unable or unwilling to embrace the unconscious side of ourselves, our awareness and understanding become limited. Lady's-Mantle facilitates the reconciliation of our outer and inner paths so that we can experience the union and wholeness which we seek, bringing to light our inherent all-knowing wisdom.

Affirmation:

I bring to light all the wisdom and awareness I need.

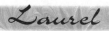

Laurel

(Prunus lusitanica)

❀ *Keynotes:* RESOURCEFULNESS and MANIFESTATION

The essence of Laurel represents the abundance of the universe. It enables those wise in heart to empower themselves to find the resources to bring their ideas and ideals into form.

❀ *Attributes:*

Unfolding the power to manifest; bringing ideas into being and putting them into action; working with the 7th Ray of organisation, order and expression of Spirit through form; ability to choose opportunities which serve one's life purpose; synthesising different facets or energies into a unified whole; evoking the power to hold and maintain silence when necessary; commitment and strength to realise one's vision.

❀ *Indications:*

Inability to 'hold the vision'; withholding of the talents; initiative and resources of the self; procrastination; giving up easily; failure to act for fear of risk-taking; failure to evoke the will to choose and then follow the way that has been determined upon; feeling overwhelmed through inability to integrate the many facets of a project; disorganisation.

The essence of Laurel has a harmonising and synthesising effect. When we bring plans to fruition, we need to be bold and to blend our energies of individuality with Higher Will. Laurel essence helps us to trust that we are supported by the spiritual world when we act for the good of the whole.

Affirmation:

I manifest all that I need to fulfil the Divine Plan. I work for the good of the whole.

(Tilia platyphyllos)

❀ *Keynotes:* ONENESS and UNIVERSALITY

Essence of Lime helps us open our hearts to the light and love of our universal being. From this awareness we experience our interrelatedness on earth and create harmonious relationships in our lives.

❀ *Attributes:*

Knowing and experiencing the self as universe; transferral from identification with lower to Higher Self; unification of individual consciousness with collective consciousness and environment; transmuting self-preservation into detached world service; humanitarian activity through recognition of need, service, relationship and sense of responsibility; group consciousness.

❀ *Indications:*

Introspection or focus on self; overidentification with lower self/personality; feeling powerless; over-dependency; fear of domination; intolerance, prejudice or nationalism; lack of awareness of the whole; separativeness.

Essence of Lime helps us to anchor universal love in our hearts. Supporting us in overcoming feelings of separation from our spiritual self or others, essence of Lime can empower and encourage us to work for peace and spiritual harmony on earth.

Affirmation:

I open my heart to create harmonious relationships in life. I am one with all other beings.

Mallow

(Lavatera sp.)

✿ *Keynotes:* ALIGNMENT and ATTUNEMENT

Mallow essence helps us to experience the unification of the mind and heart, and we learn to 'think in our hearts'. When we think and act from this fusion, we open up to God's grace.

✿ *Attributes:*

Harmonisation of thinking with feeling in the heart, leading to 'love in action'; bringing soul energies into one's thoughts and actions; the power of the unity between heart and mind; intuitive thinking through the heart; letting the heart guide; being and acting with one accord; wholeheartedness; integrity; refinement; graciousness.

✿ *Indications:*

Separation or detachment of thought from feeling; relationship conflict; discord; polarisation; being 'stuck in the head'; over-thinking; repetitive thoughts; loquaciousness; incoherence; tenaciousness; impoliteness; disorderliness; unruliness; intolerance; gaucheness.

When we create separation in our lives between our thinking and feeling, the ability to bring through Higher Will is impeded. With essence of Mallow we glory in the unification of body and soul, mind and heart, and live congruently through right relationship.

Affirmation:

I align myself with Divine Will.
I am love-in-action.

(Mimulus guttatus)

❀ *Keynotes:* PERSONAL POWER and SOUL INFUSION

Monkey Flower essence helps raise the vibrational energy from the personality level, fusing it with the soul's intention. We are empowered to celebrate and use the uniqueness of our experience and qualities to be who we truly are.

❀ *Attributes:*

Standing in one's power; evoking the soul in personal expression and empowerment; soul and personality fusion; the radiating power of the Self; the uniqueness of our personal being; acting from strength of individual purpose and with inner conviction, boldness and force of character; assertiveness; self-assurance; self-realisation; fearlessness in accepting feedback from others; ability to set clear boundaries.

❀ *Indications:*

Inability to express and act from one's truth; timidity; nervousness; apprehension; a yielding temperament: over-compliancy; being over-apologetic; giving one's power away; fear of exploitation or domination by others; patterns of dependency; fear of disapproval, blame, criticism, ridicule, humiliation; fear of another's anger or indignation; difficulty in saying no.

Sometimes we are reluctant to be fully in our power for fear of recrimination, or because we believe that in our strength or dominance we are acting from the lower self or ego. Monkey Flower essence helps us to know and trust our inner guidance and find the power and courage to act.

Affirmation:
I celebrate who I am.
I stand in my uniqueness and
truth to serve all.

Ragged Robin

(Lychnis flos-cuculi)

❀ *Keynotes:* PURITY and INNER PURIFICATION

Ragged Robin essence aids in releasing, on all levels, congestion, obstruction and toxicity and facilitates the free flow of life force and energies.

❀ *Attributes:*

Inner purification; promoting of circulation, facilitation of free flow of the life force; purgation; wholesomeness.

❀ *Indications:*

Congestion; toxicity; obstruction; blockages; unclean living; hindrance of spirit.

Pollution within ourselves and in our environment creates toxicity, congestion and obstruction to the free flow of life forces and energies. Ragged Robin essence helps us clear the channels and purify on all levels.

Affirmation:
I purify myself and clear my channels.
My energies flow free and I am restored to wholeness.

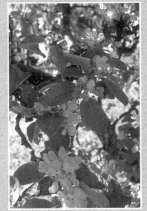

Apple

Balsam

Bell Heather

Birch

Birch trees outside the Universal Hall at the Findhorn Foundation

Broom

Daisies

Elder

Globe Thistle

Gorse overlooking Findhorn Bay

Making Gorse Essence

Grass of Parnassus

Harebells

Hazel (catkins)

Holy Thorn

Iona Pennywort

Holy Thorn outside the Community Centre, Findhorn Foundation

Lady's Mantle

Laurel

Lime

Monkey Flower

Mallow

Ragged Robin

Rose Alba

Making Rose Alba Essence

Rose Water Lily

Rowan

Scots Pine

Scottish Primrose

Sea Rocket

Silverweed

Sea Pink

Snowdrops

Spotted Orchid

Stonecrop

Sycamore

Thistle

Valerian

Watercress

Wild Pansies

Willowherb

The 'Living Machine' at the Findhorn Foundation

The Findhorn River

The original Findhorn Garden

David Spangler with Eileen and Peter Caddy, and Dorothy Maclean

Jacobite rose
(Rosa alba)

✤ *Keynotes:* WILL-TO-LOVE and OMNIPOTENCE

Rose Alba is the essence of positive, outgoing, creative expression. Through aligning Higher Mind with the Ancient Wisdom, words and action reflect the power of Universal Truth.

✤ *Attributes:*

Enlightened individual power; the creative power of the WORD; spiritual will and purpose; will-directed consciousness; divine direction and protection; positive action through intuition; ability to be self-responsible and to take initiative; leadership; ability to speak and act from inner authority; patience, persistence and perseverance; determination; strength; benevolence; honour; the masculine principle: outgoing and creative; healing with the father/father principle; virility; potency.

✤ *Indications:*

Dictatorial and authoritarian use of will; the drive for personal power and control; controlling situations or others; abuse of power; being overbearing; using words or excuses to defend, attack or justify oneself or one's actions; hiding behind self-protective shields; emotional insecurity; withholding oneself or one's expression; feeling inadequate or impotent; inability to initiate, actuate or perform; inflexibility; rigidity of ideas; strict adherence to convention or tradition; pride; arrogance; criticism; judgement; stubbornness.

Without love, power can be misused. Through learned control patterns and feelings of inadequacy or pride, the lower self or ego can undermine the inner authority of the True Self. Rose Alba assists in connecting with the Higher Self to bring forth deep inner spiritual insight and understanding, and with this comes the strength to 'walk our talk'.

Affirmation:

*I align my mind with the Ancient Wisdom
to stand in my truth.
I align my words with love and power
to speak my truth.*

Rose Water Lily

(Nymphaea sp.)

Here I am, bold and true. Forever I am yours in this Truth of Being. Purity of heart, I bring gladness. Spirit ever moving in the spiral to be — manifest here, now, forever. Courage of heart when despairing of knowing the True Self. I remind you of the Presence.

❀ *Keynotes:* PRESENCE and ASCENSION

Made from a single bloom grown in the final tank of the Living Machine*, this lily has emerged from the depths of the purified sewage, a symbol for the spirit of man, emerging out of the depths of darkest matter to ascend into the Light, radiating from the heart purity, beauty and Presence of Being.

❀ *Attributes:*

Feeling the intimate closeness and relationship to Spirit; the Beloved; spiritual evolution; spiritual poise; ascension; penetrating the mystery of the Presence through surrender.

❀ *Indications:*

Sense of loss of connection with Spirit; feeling abandoned or forsaken by God; powerless to penetrate into the depths of one's soul or spirit; losing heart when faced with difficult next steps on the Path of Return; inability to yield but desperate yearning to be delivered into Spirit.

When we fervently aspire to move on to higher levels of unfoldment or when in despair we cry out for help, essence of Rose Water Lily brings courage of heart. In faith we can descend to the depths and ascend to the heights to uncover the Truth of our Being: indestructible, immutable Spirit, our connection with the Beloved.

Affirmation:
Pure in heart and in truth I stand.
I AM.

(Sorbus aucuparia)

❀ *Keynotes:* FORGIVENESS and RECONCILIATION
Rowan essence helps us to let go of resentments and to heal old wounds.
As we learn to forgive ourselves and others, we can heal the past.

> ❀ *Attributes:*
> Ability to forgive oneself and others; learning from past experiences; resolving
> karma; harmony through conflict; releasing stored tension and pain; facing
> deep repressed emotions.

> ❀ *Indications:*
> Clinging to old behaviour patterns; judgementalness; avoidance; self-pity;
> shame; defensiveness; self-destructive patterns; unwillingness to give in and
> let go; resentment.

Rowan essence addresses our attachment to habitual, inherited or karmically
acquired emotions and patterns. By accepting the lessons of our past
experiences, we can avoid repeating mistakes and reconcile and live
congruently with ourselves and the world. Rowan opens us up to a
higher level of being and confers the power to surrender to unconditional, healing love.

Affirmation:
*I experience forgiveness
of myself and others
and surrender to
unconditional, healing
love.*

Scots Pine

(Pinus sylvestris)

❀ *Keynotes:* WISDOM and TRUTH

Scots Pine essence helps us in finding directions in our search for answers. In being open to listening, we can be guided from within by the all-knowing Self and the inner teachers.

❀ *Attributes:*

True listening; trusting one's inner knowing and intuition; hearing inner spiritual guidance; openness to the Ancient Wisdom within oneself and Nature.

❀ *Indications:*

Barriers to trusting inner knowing and intuition; blocks to inner and outer listening; resistance to hearing the truth; overdependence on outside validation; indecision.

The essence of Scots Pine helps us to clear the channels to true inner listening, and in the silence, in the seeking and asking, we can tap into our own source of wisdom within. The truth then stands revealed.

Affirmation:
I am receptive to the truth and wisdom within my being.

(Primula scotica)

❀ *Keynotes:* PEACE and UNCONDITIONAL LOVE
Essence of Scottish Primrose brings inner peace and stillness to the heart
when confronted by fear, anxiety, conflict or crisis.

❀ *Attributes:*
Inner peace and stillness; coming back to earth; inner harmony; relaxation;
purity of feeling; experience of love and compassion.

❀ *Indications:*
Fear; constriction; panic; shock; paralysis; anxiety; hysteria; inner struggle;
conflict in relationships; disheartenment.

Scottish Primrose stands for peace. When we
are afraid, anxious or in conflict, essence of
Scottish Primrose can help to restore natural
rhythms. As we find ourselves at peace,
we re-establish harmony, thereby allowing the free flow of life force to all parts
of our being, bringing equilibrium.

Affirmation:
*I am at peace in my heart
and in the world.*

Sea Pink

(Armeria maritima)

❀ *Keynotes:* HARMONY and UNIFICATION

The essence of Sea Pink aligns and infuses our being with Spirit. Blending and melding our life force with Divine Will, it helps to balance the energy flow between all energy centres.

❀ *Attributes:*

Healing the split between higher and lower selves, soul and personality; achievement of stability and balance between the opposites; harmonisation of crown and root chakras, and soul and form; surrendering the lower to the higher; will-to-be; kundalini awakening; magnetic potency which binds the soul and personality in functioning relationship.

❀ *Indications:*

Burnout or blocks in energy systems of the bodies; overload; stuckness; vacillation between the opposites; following desires of the lower self; craving stimulating experiences; untimely kundalini stimulation; split personality; the fundamental problem of the relationship between Spirit and matter.

Sea Pink essence helps us to release those lower desires or blocks which interfere with the harmonious flow of vital life force. When we feel split off from our Higher Self, essence of Sea pink helps to dissolve this barrier, and by adjusting the life and consciousness energy streams, seeks to unite the polarities within us, allowing us to follow the 'middle way'.

Affirmation:
I unite all energies within my being and welcome the balance and harmony.

(Cakile maritima)

🌸 *Keynotes:* REGENERATION and PROVIDENCE

Sea Rocket essence infuses our being with the experience of abundance in all its forms. We trust in the universal supply to receive and give freely; we act from a point of purity of purpose, knowing that all our needs will be met.

🌸 *Attributes:*

Inner knowing and trust in the abundance of Nature; reverencing and cherishing life through purity of being; tapping into the reservoir of the Self for replenishment and restoration; rehydration; succulence; ability to bring forth and sustain life; conservation of resources; fecundity.

🌸 *Indications:*

Fear of scarcity; poverty; evaporation or dissipation of one's reserves; feeling destitute; wasteful or superfluous expenditure of resources; being over-materialistic, hoarding with episodic splurging; over-protectiveness; impoverishment or depletion; surviving instead of thriving; wasting conditions; lack of absorption from the lifeblood to nourish or replenish the body; dehydration; dryness; barrenness; difficulty giving or receiving; being self-absorbed.

We may experience the feeling that we do not have sufficient resources for our needs, whether materialistic, emotional or spiritual, and this can create a constant looking outwards for the means to provide. Sea Rocket helps us to reconnect with the Laws of Manifestation and Being. When we remember that we carry the power to call forth the All out of the Nothing, we no longer need to accumulate so much to support our insecurities, and we share the abundance with an open heart.

Affirmation:

*I give and receive freely knowing that
all my needs are met.*

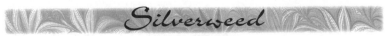

Silverweed

(Potentilla anserina)

❀ *Keynotes:* SIMPLICITY and SELF-REALISATION

Silverweed essence helps us to detach ourselves from material concerns and overindulgence, by promoting moderation and self-awareness.

❀ *Attributes:*

Awakening to spirituality; breakthrough of self-awareness; integrity; self-discipline; enjoyment of the simple pleasures of life; getting back to grass roots; moderation; frugality; humbleness.

❀ *Indications:*

Overindulgence; fussiness; pernicketiness; narrow-mindedness; disconnection from spirit; self-centredness; greed; pretentiousness.

Silverweed speaks of the necessity for living lightly on the earth. It is useful in times when we become overly engrossed in material concerns and cut off from our higher purpose or being. It allows us to get back to basics, to grass roots. It can help us to lift our awareness through deep contact with the forces of Nature and, through earthiness, to break through into higher spirituality.

Affirmation:
I live lightly on the earth and treasure all of Nature's gifts.

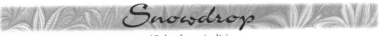

Snowdrop

(Galanthus nivalis)

✼ *Keynotes:* SURRENDER and IMMORTALITY

Snowdrop essence allows us to surrender to the final resolution of past events and attachments in life. In the death of the old we find the seed of our eternal inner light and behold new vistas.

✼ *Attributes:*

Inner radiance in times of darkness; resilience; inner strength; ability to yield; letting go as prelude to spiritual rebirth or initiation; acceptance of the processes of death leading to liberation; knowing of the Eternal Self; detachment; transcendence of the form side of life; optimism and hope for the future.

✼ *Indications:*

Personal darkness and suffering; negative or destructive attitudes; fear of death and dying; depression related to seasonal darkness (S.A.D. syndrome); dark night of the soul; grief.

The essence of Snowdrop allows us to access deep inner stillness and to surrender to the processes whereby we can release the past. Then we can see the light at the end of the tunnel and move towards it and the all-pervading presence of God, celebrating the death of the old and rejoicing in the coming of the new.

Affirmation:

I surrender and release that which has passed and rejoice in the coming of the new.

Spotted Orchid

(Dactylorhiza fuchsii)

❀ *Keynotes:* PERFECTION and CREATIVE EXPRESSION

Spotted Orchid enables us to go beyond pessimism and self-interest to seeing the best in everyone and everything.

❀ *Attributes:*

Self-expression, nurturing and creativity; positive outlook; inspiration; ability to see the beauty in life.

❀ *Indications:*

Cynicism; self-centredness; pessimism; inability to see beyond oneself and personal circumstances; nostalgia; stuckness.

When we become too focused on ourselves or our work, our vision can become limited and our outlook on life reflects this limitation. If we focus on the negative, or the ugly in life, then disillusionment or pessimism may result. Essence of Spotted Orchid allows us to see the beauty and perfection in everything, thus reflecting the beauty and perfection of our true selves. We are then able to express this creatively.

Affirmation:

I see the very best in everyone and everything.

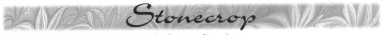

(Sedum anglicum)

❀ *Keynotes:* TRANSITION and TRANSCENDENCE

Stonecrop essence helps us to maintain inner stillness whilst in the process of breaking through inertia and resistance to change in the face of imminent transformation.

> ❀ *Attributes:*
>
> Profound self-transformation; revelation; breakthrough; self-reliance; patience; inner stillness; state of grace.
>
> ❀ *Indications:*
>
> Resistance to change; being stuck in the past; stubbornness; loneliness; isolation; inertia; stagnation.

Stonecrop aids in times of profound personal transformation, when we can sense that change is happening around us and within us at the deepest levels. It corresponds to the pupa stage of becoming a butterfly. This process has its own timing. Stonecrop essence allows us to release our attachments to the past, embrace change and find the point of stillness within.

Affirmation:

I maintain my inner stillness and calm whilst welcoming the change and transformation in my life.

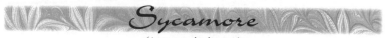

Sycamore
(Acer pseudoplatanus)

❀ *Keynotes:* SOFTNESS and REVITALISATION
Sycamore essence recharges and uplifts body and soul when we are stressed, allowing the emergence of a soft, yet powerful, new energy supply.

❀ *Attributes:*

Ability to tap inner reserves of strength; patience; constancy; endurance and persistence; continuity of effort; catalysing energy; restoring gentleness and smoothness in our energy flow; surrendering strain; conflict or anxiety; setting boundaries; encouragement when facing challenges, tests or trials; enthusiasm; softness and openness; ability to be flexible and resilient under stress.

❀ *Indications:*

Profound fatigue and exhaustion; becoming worn down over time by effort or overexertion; depletion of energies; feeling stretched to the limit; at breaking point; spiritually testing times; negative influences; bad environmental effects; heavy-heartedness; stress.

When we are worn down by time, effort or stress, our energy levels can fall and become depleted. Essence of Sycamore helps us tap into the unlimited energy source of our inner light and life force which radiates, illuminates and energises our whole being. We can then experience the smooth flow of our energies in ourselves and in life.

Affirmation:
I enjoy the smooth and gentle flow of energies in myself and in life.

Spear Thistle (Cirsium vulgare)

❀ *Keynotes:* COURAGE and SELF-EMPOWERMENT

Thistle essence helps us to find true courage in times of adversity and to respond with positive action.

> ❀ *Attributes:*
>
> Courage in the face of adversity; empowerment when facing great challenge; strength; confident action; fortitude.
>
> ❀ *Indications:*
>
> Fear; dread; threat; immobility in the face of danger; powerlessness; frightening situations, flight/fight syndrome.

When we encounter fear, our performance can be crippled. Thistle essence encourages us to access inner strength and to take appropriate action with confidence and certainty.

Affirmation:

I have the courage and strength to stand in my truth. I bring confidence and certainty into all my actions.

Valerian

(Valeriana officinalis)

❀ *Keynotes:* HUMOUR and JUBILATION

Essence of Valerian lifts our spirits and helps us to rediscover delight and happiness in living. It helps us to be at peace by taking ourselves lightly.

❀ *Attributes:*

Experiencing life wholeheartedly; contentment; sensibility; sensitivity to impression; ability to laugh at oneself; pleasure, delight and happiness in being; joyful thanksgiving; true appreciation; spontaneity.

❀ *Indications:*

Feeling weighed down by one's sense of responsibility; over-seriousness; the glamour of being busy and hard-working; hurry and worry; over-striving; stress and tension; focused too much on one's own problems; sombreness; lack of sense of fun or humour.

The essence of Valerian is uplifting to our mind, body and spirit. When we are weighed down in our busy lives by our responsibilities we can miss the simple or transient joys in life which bring us solace and happiness. Through Valerian essence we may become more responsive in the moment, lighten-up and have fun.

Affirmation:

I delight in the happiness of living and I walk my spiritual path with lightness and humour.

(Nasturtium officinale)

❀ *Keynotes:* WELLBEING and SANCTIFICATION

Watercress essence infuses into our bodies a vibrational note of purification. It can act as a powerful cleanser, stimulating our immunity, clearing stagnant energies and overcoming disease.

❀ *Attributes:*

Purification of self and environment; restoring calm, peace and restfulness; cooling the fiery desire body; clarification; elimination; purgation; miasmatic clearing; reflecting glowing good health; stimulation and strengthening of immune defences; resistance to disease through vigilance, conscientiousness and hygiene; enhancement of transformative processes; extraction of usable goodness and nutrients; purification and transformation of waste elements; drainage and discharge of dross through flushing out the systems; antisepsis; disinfection; anti-inflammatory.

❀ *Indications:*

Ill health through unhealthy or unwholesome conditions; lifestyle or environments; exposure to harmful substances or agents; unmindfulness or negligence of health or wellbeing; contamination through defilement; susceptibility to disease; miasms; low immunity; debilitation; feverish delirium; frenzy; eruptive temperament; inflammation; carrying the weight of one's transgressions.

As we travel through life our bodies absorb excesses and hold toxins derived from our emotions, lifestyle and the pollution from the environment: we may feel heavy; slowed down or become ill. Essence of Watercress helps us in refining; purifying and transforming our physical form so that the purity of our bodies reflects the light and truth of the soul.

Affirmation:
I cleanse my body and purify my soul.

Wild Pansy

(Viola tricolor)

Keynotes: RESONANCE and RADIANCE

Wild Pansy essence illuminates, clarifies and purifies the channels which connect the mind and heart. When we energise and enliven this connection, the life energies are free to flow into the heart and radiate throughout the whole being.

Attributes:

Receptivity; sensitivity and contact with higher energies; clearing the channels for energy flow, circulation and distribution, infusing mind and body with vital life energies; illumination, vibrancy, lucidity through expansiveness and receptive awareness in the heart; replenishment of the heart centre and facilitation of circulation; coordination and synergistic functioning of the thinking; feeling, and willing processes; sense of aliveness, wellbeing and balance; re-establishment of mind/body stability and connectedness.

Indications:

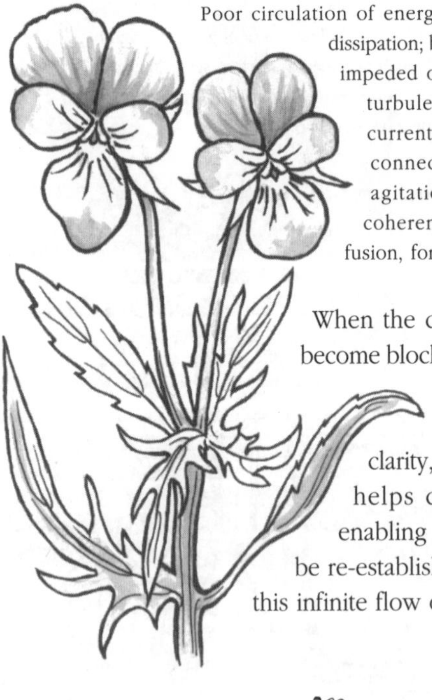

Poor circulation of energies through blockage, deviation or dissipation; blocked energy flow to the heart, being impeded or non-receptive to higher energies; turbulent, fluctuating or disturbed energy currents; sense of being detached or disconnected; spasm; tension; nervousness; agitation; tremulousness; loss of mental coherence: fogginess, distractedness, confusion, forgetfulness, disorientation.

When the channels linking the head and heart become blocked, the energies flowing through will become diverted, impeded or lost, and we may experience lack of clarity, confusion or detachment. Wild Pansy helps clear the head and the channels, enabling receptivity, sensitivity and contact to be re-established, and we register the presence of this infinite flow of energy which is Divine Love.

Affirmation:

My mind and my heart are open.
I radiate light and love.

Rosebay Willowherb
(Chamaenerion angustifolium)

❦ *Keynotes:* POWER and SELF-MASTERY

Willowherb essence helps to balance the personality that is expressing self-seeking, authoritarian or overbearing behaviour, and brings about the responsible integration of will and power issues.

❦ *Attributes:*

Integrity; self-empowerment; congruence; adept use of will; authority; self-temperance; humility; diplomacy; synergy.

❦ *Indications:*

Self-aggrandisement; self-importance; judgementalness; self-will; attachment to power and position; authoritarian behaviour; eruptive temperament; oppression; anger.

When we are attached to our positions of power, we are in danger of over-influencing or manipulating others with our willpower. We need to temper ourselves. Essence of Willowherb helps to balance force of personality with true power through humility and the correct use of the will.

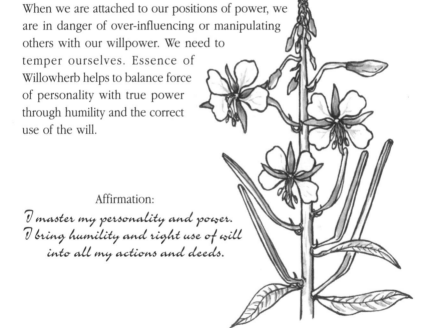

Affirmation:

I master my personality and power.
I bring humility and right use of will
into all my actions and deeds.

COMBINATION FLOWER ESSENCES

The specific properties of the individual essences are highlighted here to indicate how they work in each combination to compliment and reinforce the whole.

✢ Clear-Light ✢

Broom, River Findhorn, Wild Pansy, Birch, Scots Pine & Rose Alba

The CLEAR LIGHT Combination brings about a peaceful state of mind, mental clarity and brightness, which greatly aids in meditation. When heart, body and mind are still and aligned, a clear channel is created whereby the intuition, Higher Self and Higher (or Universal) Mind can be contacted.

Through highest aspiration one can receive inner guidance and help from the Spiritual World, and live life in accordance with one's purpose and the Divine Plan.

Broom frees the self from personality limitations.
River Findhorn helps to connect with the Source, freeing the self from personality limitations.
Wild Pansy enhances receptivity and the flow of higher wisdom into the heart.
Birch brings light to the mind and clarity of inner vision.
Scots Pine increases the ability to listen, receive inner guidance and find directions in life.
Rose Alba facilitates the positive, active expression of the guidance received.

✢ Karma-Clear ✢
Birch, Snowdrop, Rowan & Holy-Thorn

This combination aids awareness of the karmic causes of life's predicaments and ailments. Through foresight of future and understanding of past, the cause of suffering is illuminated, and attachments which bring about pain, unhappiness and disease may be released.

Birch helps to gain insight into the past and future, enabling understanding of the cause of the problem.

Snowdrop gives new hope and facilitates transition into the Light through surrender and detachment.

Rowan releases resentment and pain and heals old wounds. It supports the ability to forgive oneself and others.

Holy-Thorn opens the heart to love, acceptance, compassion and understanding.

✢ Spiritual Marriage ✢
Apple, Holy-Thorn, Mallow & Sea Pink

This combination facilitates the integration, fluidity and synthesis of the dualities found in every human being — between head and heart, mind and love, will and wisdom, male and female.

Stability and balance between the pairs of opposites, achieved through the qualities of cohesion, harmony, expansion and union, release the potential, freedom and joy of right relationship.

Apple frees the creative willpower.

Holy-Thorn opens the heart to love and intimacy and to the expression of the True Self.

Mallow assists right relationship by the graceful fusion of head and heart, mind and sentience.

Sea Pink brings harmony by balancing the energy flow between all energy centres.

✛ First Aid ✛
· · · · · · · · · · · ·
Daisy, Scottish Primrose, Bell Heather & Thistle

A soothing combination offering immediate relief in any crisis. Used in cases of stress, trauma or shock on the physical, emotional or mental level, it can help to relieve associated fear and aid in the release of tension and pain.

Daisy brings feelings of calmness, protection and centredness.
Scottish Primrose helps to anchor the life energy in the heart, and promotes relaxation and feelings of peace and love.
Bell Heather is stabilising, fostering trust and self-confidence.
Thistle gives courage to take positive action in facing any difficulty or emergency.

✛ Life-Force ✛
· · · · · · · · · · · · ·
Gorse, Elder, Sycamore, Valerian & Grass of Parnassus

LIFE FORCE is an excellent combination to help overcome tiredness, apathy and burnout. It revitalises and strengthens immunity and generates vibrancy and energy.

Gorse brings vitality, enthusiasm and joy.
Elder stimulates the body's natural powers of rejuvenation and renewal.
Sycamore helps to tap into inner reserves of strength.
Valerian serves to lift the spirits and to rediscover delight and happiness in living.
Grass of Parnassus increases the ability to receive and transform the energies which are available from the Universal Source.

✛ Revelation ✛
· · · · · · · · · · · · ·
Stonecrop, Snowdrop, Holy-Thorn & Hazel

REVELATION essence facilitates inner change and transformation. As limitations are transcended, it opens the way to a fresh flow of inspiration that restores the inner vitality needed to move forward. Through revealing the mystery of surrender and the highest personal unfoldment of the vision, comes understanding, acceptance, detachment and freedom.

Stonecrop helps to maintain inner stillness whilst in the process of breaking through inertia and resistance to change in the face of imminent transformation.

Snowdrop allows willing surrender to finding the eternal inner light that illuminates the darkness. It brings hope and the ability to behold new vistas.

Holy-Thorn opens the heart to love, acceptance, compassion and understanding.

Hazel embodies the spirit of the future. It helps one to let go of the past without grief and inspires a new vision of full creative potential.

✦ Holy Grail ✦
Balsam, Globe-Thistle, Lady's-Mantle & Rose Alba

HOLY GRAIL essence enables us to contain and embody Spirit in our physical form, hence able to share it with others. We are empowered to empty all that is unreal from the chalice of our being, and to integrate and harmonise our physical, emotional, mental and spiritual bodies, bringing them into alignment and synthesis.

When we are attuned on all levels— body, mind and soul— our essential nature is revealed and we become a vessel for the Holy Spirit.

Balsam allows us to experience love and acceptance of the physical bodies we have chosen to incarnate into as souls. We feel fully present in the world and express love and intimacy in all our relationships.

Globe-Thistle helps us willingly sacrifice non-essentials in our quest for wholeness.

Lady's-Mantle brings awareness of the infinite knowledge and wisdom available to us through the cosmos.

Rose Alba is the essence of positive, outgoing creative expression, allowing us to reflect the power of our true nature in words and action.

ESOTERIC ESSENCES

✛ Essence of Wesak ✛

Universal Hall
Wesak Full Moon, 14 May 1995

LEGEND HAS IT that at the time of the full moon in May, there is a very special gathering and ceremony held in the Wesak Valley in the Himalayas where Buddha returns each year to pour blessings upon the earth and humanity. In this ceremony, when the Buddha appears, a crystal bowl of water is blessed and the water distributed.

For our community meditation this year we felt inspired to place a crystal, bowl in the centre and at the end to share the water by way of communion.

The essence was made with the remaining water from the crystal bowl which I solarised by the light of the rising sun.

I received this message:

> *The eye is opened and now I see. Wisdom. Deep wisdom. Rejoice and absorb the energies which have been sent and let them heal all cleavages. This essence may be used in blessing and in healing, for the higher wisdom to be unfolded in time. Praise be to all who gathered to be agents for Goodwill and Peace.*

Steve Nation at the World Goodwill Wesak meeting in London that year, highlighted the opportunities offered to us at the special time of Wesak.

In the annual cycle of extra-planetary energies pouring into human consciousness Taurus provides the perfect environment for Wesak. It is an energy which brings a potency of enlightenment. 'I see and when the eye is opened all is light' — this is the keynote ... in this sign. The great gift, and opportunity hinted at here concerns the process of sight, of revelation. ... Taurus brings an energy which can stimulate the group's vision of the Plan. The goals of the Plan become clear in the group mind; the principles of wholeness, synthesis and freedom are made more alive, more tangible and real. And, as an earth sign... Taurus brings a focus on the will to serve the Plan, to manifest the vision.

✣ Exaltation ✣
· · · · · · · · · · · · · ·
Festival of Humanity, Festival of Goodwill, Festival of the Christ
Sun in Gemini, Full Moon 1995
Universal Hall, Findhorn Foundation

Flowers from all around the community, including:
Gorse, Broom, Red Poppy, Yellow Poppy, Clover, Red Campian, White Campian, Rowan, Rose, Wild Carrot, Catmint, Chives, Wild Ox-eyed Daisy, Japanese Quince, Honesty, Brassica, Lady's-Mantle, Aquilegia, Wild Borage, Vetch, Wallflower, Viper's Bugloss, Grasses, Pansy, Bluebell, The 'ten thousand things' — Buddha.

This essence was made by the whole community and came about spontaneously as we gathered for meditation to celebrate this very special festival of the Christ. Eileen Caddy led the meditation and at the end we were invited to choose a flower and to float it in a large pentagonal copper bowl. Each person sent out a prayer and a blessing into the world. Approximately a hundred and fifty blessings were infused into the essence by the gathered community.

As I sat gazing at all the beautiful flowers floating in the huge bowl in the centre, it struck me that we had created a most fantastic flower essence. I called together a group of students from the 'Touch the Earth' gardening programme I had been working with and we gathered one of each of the different flowers, along with the water, from the central bowl to make the essence.

In our attunement when collecting the essence after solarisation, the group received these inspirations:

The keynote in Gemini:

I recognise my other self and in the waning of that self, I grow and glow.

Opening the physical and inner eye to beauty as an expression of the Divine. Opening the inner and outer ear to the harmonies sounded by all flowers and living beings joined together in the charms of life. Bringing together as one in harmony and beauty.

Peace and goodwill shall reign when humanity can share blessings and love in communion with the Spirit of the One. Exalted consciousness. Embracing and radiating all the qualities of Christhood. Universal Love, Light and Wisdom. Embodying the essence of goodwill.

Blending; diversity and wholeness; clarity and inspiration; the opening of the crown chakra to become one with the universe; connecting with the divine; for embodying Christ energy, living the Christ; the heart and throat chakras open. I am Goodwill to all mankind.

For all who want to embody the Christ energy. It's not a cure, but the essence of all teachings. The time of teachings is over. This is living the Christ, the embodiment of the Christ.

ℰLEMENTAL ESSENCE
MESSAGES

The aim of his striving for knowledge about them (the nature beings) must be to create a connection between the worlds of Nature and spirit: in other words to establish a connection between nature beings and angel beings. Only a human being can make this connection, for he alone unites both realms within himself. If he withdraws from this task, both realms remain separate. The perception and understanding of nature spirits or elemental beings is essentially connected with a task which one can call 'cosmic', an evolutionary task which only human beings can accomplish, because of their special position within the cosmos.

— Rudolf Steiner

✢ Earth ✢
Findhorn River & Findhorn Nature Sanctuary, 12 July 1993

Deep within the caverns of earth we sing and work, stoking the fires that the earth may be warmed to contain the myriad life forms which inhabit this element with you, and with us. We work ceaselessly to make certain that all is brought to a fruition of the plans laid before us, wielding the power within stone and within the earth itself so that you may be warmed by the presence of the light and love of the inner sun. We are the beings of primordial creation and we give you our gift of song and merriment that you may rejoice in the very substance of your bodies, which we create from these elements. You can know us through the contact within yourselves of the deepest desire to love who you are, who we are, who have given you these bodies, which we have fashioned from within ourselves and have borne you as the fruit of our endeavours. We bring laughter and song and light-heartedness for we are beings of great density and form and structure, and yet we use the light and warmth to embody ourselves and to give us levity and lightness. Deep within we remould your desires to be free of the tethers of earth. We bring levity of beingness which will overcome inertia, through us your beings can soar to the heights, and dig deep within to find the truth of beingness on earth with us to guard you and protect you from the fires which we tend. Glory in God and glory in us, the elemental beings of earth who give ourselves to you in oneness in Her Love. Praise Be!

✣ Water ✣

The Findhorn
Findhorn River, by Randolph's Leap, 6 June 1993

I am the essence of goodness. My form extends from the highest peaks to the lowest shores and I bring purity, clarity and heavenly power which I carry in my energy streams to you, to humankind and to all beings on earth. My essence is a power beyond understanding. My keynote is supreme power and my highest aspiration is the Source. From my watery realm I bring the eternal life force of what I am: the mainspring of the heart of Christ, the channel and vessel for the holy blood. I nourish all without prejudice. My life blood is the power and strength of God, manifest, visible, tangible, nourishing you all, purifying your senses so that I may be revealed. I flow in your bloodstream, just as I flow in the bloodstream of God. I am the oneness of the watery realm and I give you sustenance and will infill your being with the infinite power of the Great Sea. I am the eternal and infinite flowing love and peace of God. The heart knows no fear. I am the supreme surrender to the power of the infinite reality of Limitless Love and Truth.

✣ Air ✣

Well of the North Wind
Sun Temple, Iona, 6 July 1994

We come in peace, spirits of the wind from the north. We guide and direct you to the shores of your sentiency where peace reigns supreme. We caress your form with the cool blue of reason. We wash over you like the blue waves that carry us forth from our Father's home and cleanse your soul so that you might receive our Father's benedictions of warmth, of light and of inspiration. We are the spirits of air clothed in the essence of water that you might be set free to soar with us to the heights. There the radiance of the sun is brought to your being by our presences. We wield the light and the warmth and carry them forth for all to share in this miracle of existence and being. We are the light of truth and we instill ourselves into your mind and heart and soul so that you might remember to honour us in His name. Praise be to the spirits of air within each one. Praise be to the One.

✛ Fire ✛

Summer Solstice Fire
The Backshore, Findhorn & Findhorn Nature Sanctuary
21 June 1993

We greet you in the warmth of togetherness and oneness. The flame has been captured in the water. A rare union, but one which is profitable to all when it occurs. The speciality of the essence of fire lies in its ability to purify and to renew. It will energise the being in a way which is not possible other than by the union of solar and fiery will. This enjoining and blending is rightfully only available to the beings who have mastered or conquered the element of fire and is now available to those who seek consciously such union within the fiery heart of matter. That I come at this time is no coincidence, for the availability of this potential opens the gateway to the many seekers who need to understand the immense opportunity now proffered.

We have joined our beings and pour out our blessings of oneness for all to see the glory of God in the eternal flame of light and love. Praise be to the Spirits of God inflaming the souls of man to see the inner flame of truth and oneness with the Infinite Sun. Glory Be!

✛ Ether ✛

Well of Eternal Youth
Dun-I, Iona, 15 August 1993

I bring peace. Peace to the soul which has journeyed far and has reached the shores of serenity by endeavour, by patience and by love. I bring the supreme surrender of the soul to the light and love of being in God. This is the surrender of the soul to Spirit, bringing absolute peace in God. I am the Holy Breath — that which you breathe into your soul is the essence of what I am. I am the spirit of truth. I am the sword of light. I am the chalice of love. I am the boundless wisdom of the sea, the infinite sea of God's wisdom, laving your form, washing upon the shores of your sentiency. I am the deep earth of your being — that stillness which only matter can know.

94   But most of all I am the fire in your heart and in your mind and in your very word. I am the I Am That I Am. I come from the Source and I nourish all. I am the All. I am the infinite unending fiery breath of God manifest in the living waters of life. I am the lifeblood of God. I am the Beloved in all things. I am life. I am Consciousness. I am the peace of God descended upon man in benediction and in praise of this my most precious creation — my stewards of earth.

FLOWER ESSENCE MESSAGES

✛ Apple ✛

Findhorn Nature Sanctuary, Beltane Eve and May Day morning, 1993

MY KEYNOTE is discipline, that necessary ingredient to a life of service to the Most High and to all earth's minions and dominions. I bring opportunity. This is a joyful day, when what I am can be accepted as the process of purifying the bodies so that the new may be born and emerge out of it. I am power and I am will. Give me your self and I will remould your desires into the highest aspiration — the will-to-truth.

✛ Balsam ✛

(Impatiens glandulifera)
Findhorn Garden, 19 July 1994

Glory be, for I come to bring my Father's essence into the womb of matter. I am love born and made fruitful in your breast, in your heart and in the depths of your feminine soul. Deep within the confines of darkest, lushest dampness I am born and I unite with you so that the essence of what I am can be borne forth. I foster and nurture human love. I am the sacrifice of the self to the Highest that the son might be born from the union of heaven and earth. I draw you into my depths and I enfold you with the precious feelings of love. This is the love of being, of matter in divine manifestation, revealing the Goddess and inviting all into her womb of wonder and embrace. I am the womb of creation. Let my seeds scatter forth to fertilise the barrenness of your souls and reveal me in the darkest depths. Praise the father and the mother. May they unite and live in harmony and bear the fruit of my eternal bliss and creativity. Praise be to the son who is born from this union. Hail to the Christ child within.

✢ Birch ✢

Findhorn Nature Sanctuary, Ascension Day, 20 May 1993

I am the angel of hope for the future. My being extends into the vastness of space and time yet to come. I am there in oneness with the past and the present and the future. Through what I am you can transcend the time and space of this reality, travel to lands beyond and before. There you will find what I am — the glory of God manifest within all the universe to be seen and felt and heard and touched and tasted. I am the all-pervading vastness of time and space where universes meet and Gods play.

✢ Elder ✢

Findhorn Nature Sanctuary, 19 June 1993

The sweetness that I am is energising your being. It brings joys and gladness to the heart, and to the senses to behold what I am — sweet eternal youth. I rejuvenate and I enlighten the being on all levels. I stimulate and facilitate action in response to what I touch within the deepest innermost core. That quality is beauty in the eye of the beholder. Praise be, for you have brought me forth to share my gifts when the earth needs to open up to the infinite beauty of God.

✢ Globe-Thistle ✢

(Echinops sphaerocephalus)
Cullerne Garden, 26 July 1994

Every being and every kingdom sacrifices itself unto the higher. Thus all move up in the realms in order and in dance. This spirit of surrender to the higher order can be a happy occasion, the acknowledgement that the sacrifice of the self can be consciously undertaken in deepest joy and peace. The pain of letting go is but small recompense for the liberation of spirit, soul and body in giving to the whole of evolution. All is wholeness. We are one. The earth is one and will sacrifice itself as will the sun (son). All flows in order and the spheres are balanced, until the balance is tipped and the next spiral appears. Such is the spiral of life and consciousness in man, in universes, in all that exists.

On moonbeams of love we arise and bring to you supreme joy in beholding the sublime perfection of earthly and heavenly conjoining, serenity and absolute peace through joy, and through the transmutation of power into love. Such an alchemical process requires the cool light of the reflected sun. Delicacy, sweet femininity, gentleness and subtlety. My presence illuminates the unconscious desires and brings them into the light of day. There the light plays games with my form, filtering the powerful sun rays, extracting the power and diffusing it until it has been stepped down to a gentle flow and vibration capable of being used by the delicate, the weak, the soft and the new. Love is born in the heart. Light is extracted in useable proportion and condensed into pure love. (The power of love is a most valuable asset for it empowers those with the need for 'spiriting' to be in truth and light and to let this power touch all.) Unfold my power and love within you.

Open to the expression of who I am and to my unfoldment within you of bliss and peace, power and love in the sweetest form available to you. I unfold myself to reveal all possibilities. I heal your soul when powerful feelings weigh you down to earth and I uplift you so that you may unfold the love in your heart and mind and soul and let it express through all the forms of (your) Nature. My gift is perpetual serenity and grace. Rejoice and give thanks to the waters of life which bring me forth and revel in my presence like children dancing in the rain. Let me wash over you and bring you my peace and joy.

✢ Hazel ✢

(Corylus avellana)
River Findhorn by Sluie and the Findhorn Nature Sanctuary
12 March 1995

I am the overseer of the future unfoldment of your true potential. I help to unfold your being like the petals of a flower to the infinite possibilities of your divine birthright. You are the seed bursting forth the fullest possibility of the God manifest on the earthly plane. I cause the shattering of the shells which retain you within the form of your own mind structure. I shatter the bonds which bind you to the past. I scatter the pieces without grief, only the spirit of new unfoldment and growth remains to soothe like a balm the aching reminders of what has gone. Surrender with joy. Cast off your shackles and cares and take a leap into the river of life. Let it carry you onward into new life, new birth and new creation. I am the Spirit of the Future. Look not back but move forward with vision and wisdom gained from the experiences past. Let the heart speak out the truth of what is to come when the fear of surrendering has passed into the joy and bliss of freedom. We greet you in the wonder and joy of newness. Spring to life and rejoice in the ever-changing rhythm and trust the power of the infinite movement of the cosmic waters. Let life flow free.

✛ Holy Thorn ✛

Findhorn Nature Sanctuary, Easter Sunday morning, 1993

Within mankind the birth of the Christ is manifest through what I am. I have the power and the love to transform . From a state of grace I am born in the heart. The unfoldment of what I am is made visible in the transformation of the being from a state of sleeping to a state of dreaming. This transition signifies an awakening within the deep subconscious of the Light and Love of Truth — the reality of my being heralding the coming of the Christ energies into the hearts and minds of man. I am the total infusion of the love of Christ born in the heart of man. Be what I am — Love. I am born when the womb has been made fruitful, when the time is ripe the Christ is born from the union of heaven and earth, man and woman, heart and mind. That is the essence of what I am. The body is resurrected and I am born — SPIRIT IN MAN and MAN IN SPIRIT. My highest aspiration is Creation — the WORD of God made manifest on earth.

✛ Iona Pennywort ✛

(umbilicus rupestris)
Druid Temple, Iona
Flowers from darkness solarised in Hermit's Cell
Flowers in sunlight solarised at White Strand, Traigh Bhan
Water from the Well of the North Wind
8 July 1996

I bring my light into the crevices where seeming darkness dwells. But in truth the darkness coexists to reveal the Truth of beingness. You do not care for the darkness. Therefrom spring your fears of the unknown. The dweller of the threshold may await you at any turning, so why hide and pretend it cannot be now, here and now? Demons of the mind may claim your thoughts but remember always the Truth.

Holy Spirit come to me and fill me with the grace of Your Presence that I may be whole and seek my Beloved where'er he be, even in the shadow of the night. Bless us with the eyes to see and know the Lover (Beloved) in the heart of the flame which is succoured in the womb of darkest matter. He whom you call Satan is but the reflection of the Almighty in manifestation of the dark powers. Fear not the underworld of form, for there dwells he whom you would know in yourself. Glory in the almighty presence of the Light in formless form.

✦ Lady's Mantle ✦
(Alchemilla vulgaris)
The sunlight essence
Findhorn Garden, 19 July 1994

I am the mantle of the heavens and I represent the starry cosmos. We shine by night but our mysteries are withheld in the light of day. This serves to prevent the wisdom of the stars being captured by those who are not yet ready to encompass the All within the heart and mind and being. We reflect the wisdom of the ages. We allow you to surrender to this knowing. Let our light shine upon you to illuminate the depths of the unconscious. There you will find your other self, which you fear and which will set you free. This is our gift, the surrender to infinite love and power flowing from the cosmos into your being to show you the way to the starry realms of inner being and wholeness. We greet you in the warmth of our father sun who is the bridegroom to the heavenly mother of the cosmos whom we celebrate within your heart. Glory in us and have no fear for the infinite realities are yours for the taking.

The moonlight essence
Findhorn Garden, Full Moon, 22 July 1994

The moonlight enhances my presence within your being, to bring the unconscious into the light of day. This will serve you in understanding the cosmic connections of your inner and outward paths so they may be reconciled. When these two meet but do not cross there is a relationship set up between them causing a radiatory force field . This all-powerful force field will draw into itself all that wishes for union and wholeness and will radiate it forth affecting everything it touches. Such is the magnetism of the Christ love and light. May the love and power of the Mother overshadow you and bring peaceful birth to your whole and True Self.

(Lady's-Mantle essence is made by blending the sunlight and moonlight essences)

✣ Laurel ✣
. . . .
Cluny Hill Power Point & Findhorn Nature Sanctuary, 9 July 1993

I am a being which represents the wealth of the cosmos. This wealth comes out of my being and can be acknowledged and used by only the wise in heart. I deliver God's prosperity to the universe, and on the earth I shower you all with my divine petals, which fall upon the ground and nourish the earth; my seeds are blown in the wind and so you all prosper. Hail to the Gods of Goodness, the ever-present understanding that the wealth of the universe is ours for the giving and the sharing.

✣ Lime ✣
. . . .
Findhorn Nature Sanctuary
Consecration of Universal Sanctuary, 22 July 1993

Oneness with the Spirit of Universality is my keynote. I come to you in the ever faithful knowing that this oneness is the key to unlocking your True Self. I come this day in remembrance of the ever-flowing truth and light of the Beloved, the knowing of this will allow this Presence to infill the being and illuminate it with the presence of the universal love of God. You are already aware that this spirit has been anchored here this day. Now I come to herald the birth of this consciousness here and now. The planet earth is awakening to the reality of the love and light of Christ. Now I manifest the cosmic connections of this reality on Earth so that all may know that this presence is here, alive and flowing in the bloodstreams of all living things, least of all you humans who carry within the heart the resources to make this a reality.

I bring strength of character, perseverance and those qualities which will allow the strength of Spirit to illuminate the being so that nought but love and light will over-light it with the Presence of what I represent. All-Knowing God — the universality of my presence for all to see the ultimate power force of the Infinite Universal Being of God. Blessed are those who can see the light and love of God the Beloved in all creation. Blessed are those who know God in their hearts and minds. Blessed are those who can accept this reality and have it move them into the infinite reality of universality.

✛ Mallow ✛

(Lavatera sp)
Findhorn Garden, 17 November 1995
(33rd Anniversary of the Findhorn Foundation)

You feel my presence settle into your heart. Can you think in your heart? This is the goal for you and for all humanity — to reflect in the heart the mind of God in action and activity. Thereby the Will of God becomes enforced and manifest on the physical plane of being. This marriage must occur before the soul can descend in full measure for the unification of soul and body, and mind and heart. As a functioning whole, you manifest the Beloved in actuality. Such a fusion is by Divine Grace. We give you Divine Grace by our presence within you. Praise be this day and glory to the beings of the angelic realms who unite with you as you achieve your own unity. Glory in the unity of all beings.

✛ Monkey Flower ✛

(Mimulus guttatus)
Living Machine, Findhorn, 13 June 1996
(using Findhorn 33rd Anniversary water)

Let the power and the strength of the sun illuminate the self. Let it speak 'THIS IS WHO I AM'. The force of personality fusing with the soul speaks powerfully throughout the being without fear of recrimination. So shall it be when I am present and guiding you to be as fully aware as you can be, empowered and acting in accordance with the Plan, despite all concern that the self may be dominant. Let My dominance be. Trust and know that this is the Plan. Forcefulness and power to act NOW, in this moment, allowing my presence to pervade the All.

✛ Rose Alba ✛

Jacobite Rose
(Rosa alba)
Findhorn Garden, Leo Full Moon, 21 July 1994

I am the mouthpiece of God. I am the Ancient One. I am all-knowing. I hold the sacred sceptre and I hold the sacred sword. I am the King of Creation. I am the power of the universe. I am the father incarnate.

✢ Rose Water Lily ✢

Living Machine, Findhorn
Using Wesak Water
Gemini Full Moon, 1 June 1996

Here I am, bold and true. Forever I am yours in this Truth of Being. Purity of heart, I bring gladness. Spirit ever moving in the spiral to be — manifest here, now, forever. Courage of heart when despairing of knowing the True Self. I remind you of the Presence. Eternally yours in the Spirit of Truth and Being.

✢ Rowan ✢

Findhorn Nature Sanctuary, 8 June 1993

My bittersweet petals reveal the reality of this duality — that sweetness comes after the bitter taste of pain has passed the understanding of the wrong doing, which caused the wound to fester and require cleansing. This quality of learning through difficulty is in line with the thoughts of 'harmony through conflict'. Humanity treads this path at this time, and my essence will allow and permit an understanding when, in the time of crisis, understanding will bring insight and the power to surrender, to let go of the resistance to change. Patterns can be built, or broken and the fragments reused in the building of new and correct thought-forms to be manifest in accordance with the Divine Plan. I am with you always in your endeavours to purify and cleanse the bodies of all that does not reflect the light and love and wisdom of the Divine Plan. I am your bridge to understanding and self-forgiveness.

✢ Scots Pine ✢

Findhorn Nature Sanctuary, 7–8 June 1993

My essence is the primordial force of Nature, ancient wisdom retained in my form. Now my wisdom is here for all to share in the infinite wisdom which is God's gift to you all. This wisdom is ever present, has always been present, and will allow the soul to contact that ancient stream of knowledge which is the All-Knowing. My power is available to those who seek to contact the secret teachings within the Self, and within Nature. This ability is now offered to the humble and the true, even though the mind may seem incapable or unable to hold and contain it. I bring clarity of insight, foresight, hindsight and all this simultaneously in the twinkling of an eye. I am the ancient Truth of God, recreated to bridge the past and the future into the eternal Now.

✢ Sea Pink ✢

Balfour Bay, Isle of Erraid, 27 May 1993

My keynote is supreme surrender to the forces of (Divine) Will. This is the will-to-be, that quality of beingness for which you all strive, and yet which cannot be achieved by striving; but merely by the will of God-to-BE can it be realised. My highest aspiration is sacrifice to God — the giving of oneself in full knowing; in complete love and acceptance of the oneness of the self with the all else, all beingness. This sacrifice, which is asked of each one of us, is known to the beings of the Infinite, who give themselves absolutely and in totality, in love and joy of enjoining with the myriad builders and workers of Light. You are no different, but in the seeking to fulfil the wants and desires of your little selves you lose sight of this until providence returns you to the fold. My essence brings you peace of mind in this knowing, that we are one in this work, and that together all can be achieved in love.

✢ Sea Rocket ✢

White Strand, Iona, 10 July 1996

I have the power to exist despite the apparent destitution of the environment. The mineral silica feeds me with all that I require. I transform the elements into the lifeblood which feeds the systems. Dryness is transformed into succulent flesh. I cherish all that is given and with frugality transform the smallest seed into abundant blessings of life. Purity of purpose is the aim, then the path stands clear without need for self-furnishment along the way. Trust in the universal supply to give what is rightfully and truly ours. All that we receive and all that we give is God-given, as in the beginning. I sound the note which calls forth the power to manifest out of the Nothing, the All. You carry this power within you, use it wisely and with reverence for all creation. Share the abundance with a frugal heart for self.

✢ Snowdrop ✢

Findhorn Garden, 20 February 1994

Rejoice, rejoice, rejoice, for I have come to herald the birth of the new. Cast away the old and embrace the destruction of the old decaying forms which no longer serve. I am the new, resurrected out of the embers of that fiery love which is what I am. I have two faces, one so horrible you would not know me there as God, and one so profound you cannot conceive it or believe it. I am the immortal fiery essence of God, instilled in the heart of man, of animal, of plant, of all that lives and breathes and moves and thinks itself into being. I am life. I am death. I am the fiery breath of God which creates and destroys by the Divine Will. I separate and divide, I bind and I loosen and I coalesce the energies of the substance which is the kernel of immortal life. I am the eternal flame.

✦ Sycamore ✦

Findhorn Nature Sanctuary, 9 May 1994

You sense and feel my light radiating out from my centre in all directions, like the rays of the sun warming, illuminating, revealing, I come into your being. I bring strength when the soul has become worn by effort over time, where the tides of life have worn away the rough edges to a smooth and silken finish, but you feel as though there is nought left but the mass of concentrated being. Then I come to uplift you. The old has been left behind. The new is unrecognisable and here is the key — to find the essence of what remains and to infuse it with the will of the self so that the new emergence will blossom and flow out of the remains of the old. This quality is softness. Softness with the firm tenacity of soul guiding. Smoothness with the knowledge of what has been smoothed, the labour of love which has rounded out the being to something of beauty and wholeness. My keynote is softness and I strive for flexibility — to be open and flowing in the river of light and love which is God in the body of man.

✦ Valerian ✦

Findhorn River and Findhorn Nature Sanctuary
Full Moon, 2 August 1993

I bring supreme happiness when you are weighed down by the sense of responsibility. Then I come to uplift you and to give you a peaceful return to the true being that you are, fun loving, joyful and light, enjoying your pastime on earth and revelling in the presence of this lightness of being which is all that I am. Know me in the laughter of children, know me in the bird's song, know me in the rushing of the river, for I bring you peace of mind, peace of heart, peace of being.

My keynote is fun and my highest aspiration is humour. This humour is always lying beneath all that you do and think and say. I allow you to express this God-given gift so that the world may be uplifted and so that God may be remembered and seen in a joke, a ditty, a pun, or just in a smile.

You know me already — now bring me forth and enlighten your life and the lives of all you meet by invoking my presence so that all may know that God is love and love is laughter, joy, supreme idealism manifest in the merriment of man. Rejoice and sing praises to God for all that you have to be glad of and remember me when the travails of life bring you to your knees in thanksgiving for the joy which is waiting to be brought forth for all to share.

✢ Watercress ✢

(Nasturtium officinale)
Living Machine
Gemini Full Moon, 1 June, 1996

(I bring)... integrity of being through the purification of self and environment, allowing fullness of being to shine. The light of truth reveals the darkness – the purity of the depths is seen in full measure so to be held, incorporated, as part of the whole. Washing away the dross, leaving the channels clean and a pure reflection of the light of truth. So it is and is so realised. Cooling down the fire of desire, I bring restfulness and flowing grace of presence. Know me in the depths of your being and allow your self to surrender to the wonder and perfection which is God's glory in the manifested world of form and being. Flow with me to the pure source of the all.

✢ Wild Pansy ✢

(Viola tricolor)
Findhorn Garden, Full Moon, 23 June 1994

Glory in my vibrancy. Glory in my radiatory powers, for I clear your head and I link with your heart and so a clear channel is created whereby the divine flowing energies are freely available and energising the being. I illuminate also, clarify and purify all in one action so that you might be receptive to these energies which hitherto were unavailable due to a static condition whereby the flow is impeded and diverted, or divided and so lost to its purpose — the purpose being to energise and enliven the connection so that receptivity, sensitivity and contact can be realised. This you will achieve through the essence of what I am. I open your eyes, your heart and your mind to the infinite flow of Divine Love into the centre of your being. There it enters the blood and infuses it with life and is then distributed far and wide so that the whole being registers my presence. Yea, my presence pervades the All. Know yourself. Be yourself.

$\mathcal{I}$ NDEX OF QUALITIES, ATTRIBUTES & INDICATIONS

Abandonment	Balsam, Rose Alba, Stonecrop
Absent-mindedness	Birch, Broom, Lady's-Mantle, Wild Pansy
Abuse of power	Rose Alba, Willowherb
Abundance	Harebell, Laurel, Sea Rocket
Acceptance	Balsam, Elder, Globe-Thistle, Holy-Thorn, Rowan
Accidents, trauma	First Aid
Action	Apple, Hazel, Laurel, Rose Alba, Thistle
Addiction	Apple, Globe-Thistle, Hazel, Snowdrop
Aging	Daisy, Elder, Sycamore
Aggression	Lime, Monkey Flower, Rose Alba, Willowherb, Thistle
Alienation	Balsam, Holy Thorn, Lime, Rose Water Lily, Stonecrop
Alignment	Apple, Harebell, Mallow, Rose Alba, Clear Light, Holy Grail
Aliveness	Elder, Gorse, Wild Pansy, Life Force
Aloofness	Balsam, Grass of Parnassus, Holy Thorn, Rose Alba, Stonecrop
Amends	Iona Pennywort, Globe-Thistle, Holy-Thorn, Rowan
	Scottish Primrose, Karma Clear
Ancient Wisdom	Scots Pine, Rose Alba, Clear Light
Anger	Monkey Flower, Rowan, Willowherb
Anguish	Iona Pennywort, Rose Water Lily, Scottish Primrose,
	Sycamore
Anxiety	Monkey Flower, Scottish Primrose, Sycamore, Thistle
Apathy	Gorse, Lady's-Mantle, Life Force
Approval	Balsam, Holy-Thorn, Monkey Flower
Arrogance	Lime, Rose Alba, Willowherb
Assertiveness	Apple, Bell Heather, Hazel, Monkey Flower, Rose Alba, Thistle
Attachment	Apple, Harebell, Hazel, Rowan, Sea Rocket, Stonecrop
	Karma Clear
Attention	Broom, Daisy, Lady's-Mantle, Wild Pansy
Attunement	Globe-Thistle, Grass of Parnassus, Mallow, Rose Alba, Scots Pine,
	Holy Grail
Authority	Monkey Flower, Rose Alba, Willowherb
Avoidance	Hazel, Iona Pennywort, Rowan, Karma Clear
Awareness	Birch, Lady's-Mantle, Iona Pennywort, Holy Grail, Scots Pine,
	Wild Pansy, Clear Light
Balance	Globe-Thistle, Harebell, Sea Pink, Wild Pansy, Spiritual Marriage
Barriers	Balsam, Grass of Parnassus, Holy Thorn, Iona Pennywort, Lady's-
	Mantle, Monkey Flower, Rose Alba, Rowan

Beauty	Elder, Grass of Parnassus, Rose Water Lily, Spotted Orchid
Bereavement	Grass of Parnassus, Hazel, Snowdrop
Birth	Balsam, Grass of Parnassus, Hazel, Holy-Thorn
Bitterness	Rowan, Scottish Primrose, Karma Clear
Blame	Monkey Flower, Rose Alba, Rowan, Karma Clear
Blocks	Ragged Robin, Sea Pink, Watercress, Wild Pansy
Boldness	Apple, Hazel, Monkey Flower, Rose Alba
Bonding	Balsam, Holy-Thorn, Spiritual Marriage
Bossiness	Rose Alba, Willowherb
Boundaries	Balsam, Globe-Thistle, Grass of Parnassus, Hazel, Monkey Flower, Stonecrop, Sycamore
Breakthrough	Hazel, Holy-Thorn, Snowdrop, Stonecrop
Brokenhearted	Grass of Parnassus, Holy-Thorn, Rowan, Scottish Primrose, Karma Clear
Burnout	Elder, Gorse, Sea Pink, Sycamore, Wild Pansy, Life Force
Calmness	Bell Heather, Daisy, Scottish Primrose, Watercress, First Aid
Causes	Birch, Rowan, Karma Clear
Caring	Balsam, Globe-Thistle, Holy-Thorn
Catharsis	Ragged Robin, Rowan, Watercress, Willowherb, Karma Clear
Centredness	Daisy, Globe-Thistle, First Aid
Chakras:	
Crown	Globe-Thistle, Exaltation, Rose Alba, Snowdrop
Ajna/Third Eye	Birch, Broom, Scots Pine, Wesak Blessing, Wild Pansy
Throat	Apple, Exaltation, Holy-Thorn, Laurel
Heart	Exaltation, Holy-Thorn, Mallow, Rose Water Lily, Scottish Primrose
Solar Plexus	Gorse, Monkey Flower, Silverweed
Sacral	Apple, Balsam, Sea Rocket, Willowherb
Base	Sea Pink, Thistle
Challenges	Bell Heather, Iona Pennywort, Snowdrop, Sycamore, Thistle, First Aid
Change	Hazel, Snowdrop, Stonecrop, Revelation
Channelling	Birch, Rose Alba, Scots Pine, Wild Pansy, Clear Light
Channels	Ragged Robin, Scots Pine, Sea Pink, Wild Pansy, Clear Light
Child	Bell Heather, Daisy, Grass of Parnassus, Valerian
City-living stress	Daisy, Bell Heather, Grass of Parnassus, Valerian, Wild Pansy, Sycamore
Clarity	Birch, Broom, Mallow, Scots Pine, Sea Rocket, Wild Pansy, Clear Light
Cleansing	Ragged Robin, Watercress
Co-dependency	Balsam, Globe-Thistle, Hazel, Monkey Flower, Rowan, Watercress, Karma Clear
Commitment	Apple, Laurel, Hazel, Rose Alba
Communication	Broom, Lady's-Mantle, Rose Alba, Wild Pansy, Clear Light
Community	Apple, Globe-Thistle, Laurel, Lime
Compassion	Globe-Thistle, Holy-Torn, Scottish Primrose, Karma Clear
Comprehension	Lady's-Mantle, Lime, Mallow, Clear Light

Concentration	Broom, Lady's-Mantle, Wild Pansy, Clear Light
Confidence	Bell Heather, Monkey Flower, Thistle
Confidentiality	Laurel
Conflict	Bell Heather, Grass of Parnassus, Mallow, Rowan, Scottish Primrose, Sycamore, First Aid
Confusion	Birch, Broom, Daisy, Wild Pansy
Co-operation	Lady's-Mantle, Lime, Mallow
Coordination	Broom, Lady's-Mantle, Wild Pansy
Congestion	Holy-Thorn, Ragged Robin, Scottish Primrose, Stonecrop, Watercress, Wild Pansy
Congruence	Globe-Thistle, Mallow, Rowan, Willowherb
Constriction	Holy-Thorn, Scottish Primrose, Stonecrop, Wild Pansy
Control	Daisy, Hazel, Rose Alba, Willowherb
Courage	Iona Pennywort, Rose Water Lily, Scottish Primrose, Thistle, First Aid
Craving	Apple, Globe-Thistle, Iona Pennywort, Sea Pink
Creativity	Holy-Thorn, Rose Alba, Spotted Orchid
Crisis	Bell Heather, Scottish Primrose, Thistle, First Aid
Criticism	Monkey Flower, Rose Alba, Rowan, Spotted Orchid, Willowherb
Cynicism	Mallow, Lime, Spotted Orchid
Darkness	Iona Pennywort, Snowdrop, Rose Water Lily
Dark night of the soul	Iona Pennywort, Rose Water Lily, Snowdrop, Thistle
Daydreaming	Birch, Daisy, Lady's-Mantle
Death	Iona Pennywort, Rose Water Lily, Snowdrop, Stonecrop
Decisions	Broom, Scots Pine, Clear Light
Defensiveness	Rose Alba, Rowan, Willowherb
Dejection	Balsam, Holy-Thorn
Delusion	Birch, Broom, Iona Pennywort, Wild Pansy, Clear Light
Denial	Iona Pennywort
Dependency	Globe-Thistle, Lime, Monkey Flower
Depletion	Gorse, Elder, Sea Rocket, Sycamore, Life Force
Depression	Holy-Thorn, Iona Pennywort, Snowdrop, First Aid
Desire	Apple, Balsam, Iona Pennywort, Sea Pink
Despair	Iona Pennywort, Rose Water Lily, First Aid
Destiny	Hazel
Destructiveness	Rowan, Snowdrop
Detachment	Globe-Thistle, Hazel, Rowan, Snowdrop, Karma Clear, Revelation
Determination	Apple, Hazel, Monkey Flower, Rose Alba
Direction	Bell Heather, Birch, Hazel, Scots Pine, Wild Pansy, Clear Light
Disconnection	Scots Pine, Sea Pink, Silverweed, Wild Pansy
Discouragement	Globe-Thistle, Hazel, Scottish Primrose, Sycamore
Discipline	Apple, Globe-Thistle, Iona Pennywort, Rose Alba, Silverweed
Discrimination	Iona Pennywort, Lime, Rose Alba
Dissipation	Lady's-Mantle, Sea Rocket, Wild Pansy
Divorce	Hazel, Holy-Thorn, Snowdrop, Stonecrop, Revelation; Spiritual Marriage + Snowdrop
Dogmatism	Birch, Mallow, Rose Alba

Domination	Lime, Monkey Flower, Rose Alba
Dreams	Birch, Iona Pennywort, Lady's-Mantle
Dreamers	Daisy, Lady's-Mantle, Wild Pansy
Drugs, addictions	Apple, Daisy, Globe-Thistle, Sea Pink
Dullness	Birch, Broom, Gorse, Elder, Sycamore, Valerian, Wild Pansy
Dutifulness	Apple, Globe-Thistle, Rose Alba
Dyslexia	Broom, Lady's-Mantle
Earthiness	Balsam, Bell Heather, Sea Rocket, Silverweed
Effectiveness	Apple, Hazel, Monkey Flower
Elimination	Grass of Parnassus, Hazel, Ragged Robin, Stonecrop, Watercress
Eloquence	Holy Thorn, Mallow, Rose Alba
Emergence, spiritual	Iona Pennywort, Rose Water Lily, Sea Pink, Spiritual Marriage, First Aid
Emergency	Bell Heather, Scottish Primrose, Thistle, First Aid
Emotional body	Bell Heather, Daisy, Grass of Parnassus, Rowan
Empowerment	Apple, Grass of Parnassus, Laurel, Monkey Flower, Rose Alba, Willowherb, Thistle
Enchantment	Iona Pennywort
Endurance	Globe-Thistle, Snowdrop, Sycamore, Thistle
Energy	Gorse, Elder, Sea Pink, Wild Pansy, Life Force
Enjoyment	Balsam, Elder, Daisy, Gorse, Hazel, Valerian, Revelation
Enthusiasm	Gorse, Elder, Sycamore, Valerian, Life Force
Enlightenment	Wesak Blessing, Rose Alba, Rose Water Lily, Clear Light
Escapism	Birch, Globe-Thistle, Lady's-Mantle
Estrangement	Balsam, Holy-Thorn, Mallow, Rowan, Scottish Primrose, Stonecrop
Evil	Daisy, Iona Pennywort, Thistle
Exhaustion	Gorse, Elder, Sycamore, Watercress, Life Force
Exhibitionism	Balsam
Expression	Holy Thorn, Monkey Flower, Rose Alba, Spotted Orchid
Failure	Bell Heather, Gorse, Hazel, Valerian
Faith	Bell Heather, Hazel, Harebell, Rose Water Lily, Sea Rocket
Faithfulness	Balsam, Grass of Parnassus, Globe-Thistle, Spiritual Marriage
Fanaticism	Iona Pennywort, Lime, Rose Alba, Willowherb
Fastidiousness	Silverweed, Valerian
Father	Rose Alba
Fatigue	Gorse, Elder, Sea Pink, Sycamore, Valerian, Life Force
Fault-finding	Monkey Flower, Rowan, Willowherb
Fear	Iona Pennywort, Scottish Primrose, Thistle, First Aid
Feminine	Balsam, Grass of Parnassus, Sea Rocket
Fertility	Balsam, Grass of Parnassus, Holy-Thorn, Sea Rocket
Fickleness	Balsam, Daisy, Grass of Parnassus
Finances	Harebell, Laurel, Sea Rocket
First Aid	First Aid
Flexibility	Globe-Thistle, Hazel, Rose Alba, Sycamore
Focus	Birch, Broom, Lady's-Mantle, Mallow, Wild Pansy
Forgetfulness	Birch, Broom, Daisy, Lady's-Mantle, Scots Pine, Wild Pansy

Forgiveness	Holy-Thorn, Rowan, Scottish Primrose, Karma Clear
Fortitude	Bell Heather, Globe-Thistle, Iona Pennywort, Snowdrop, Stonecrop, Sycamore
Freedom	Globe-Thistle, Hazel, Snowdrop, Revelation
Frigidity	Balsam, Gorse, Daisy, Elder, Grass of Parnassus, Holy-Thorn
Frugality	Sea Rocket, Silverweed
Frustration	Hazel, Monkey Flower, Rose Alba, Spotted Orchid, Stonecrop
Fulfilment	Apple, Hazel, Laurel, Monkey Flower
Fun	Daisy, Gorse, Valerian, Revelation
Fusion	Mallow, Monkey Flower, Spiritual Marriage
Gentleness	Balsam, Grass of Parnassus, Holy-Thorn, Sycamore
Glamour	Daisy, Elder, Iona Pennywort
Goals	Apple, Hazel, Monkey Flower, Rose Alba
Goodwill	Globe-Thistle, Exaltation, Holy-Thorn, Lime, Wesak Blessing
Grace	Daisy, Grass of Parnassus, Mallow, Stonecrop
Greed	Globe-Thistle, Harebell, Sea Rocket, Silverweed
Grief	Globe-Thistle, Grass of Parnassus, Snowdrop, First Aid, Revelation
Grounding	Balsam, Bell Heather, Daisy, Scottish Primrose, First Aid
Groups	Laurel, Lime, Scottish Primrose
Group consciousness	Apple, Globe-Thistle, Laurel, Lime, Exaltation
Guilt	Iona Pennywort, Rowan
Habits	Apple, Globe-Thistle, Iona Pennywort, Sea Rocket, Silverweed, Watercress
Happiness	Daisy, Gorse, Valerian
Harmony	Balsam, Lime, Mallow, Rowan, Sea Pink, Revelation, Spiritual Marriage
Hate	Balsam, Holy-Thorn, Lime, Scottish Primrose, Rowan, Karma Clear
Heaviness	Elder, Gorse, Stonecrop, Sycamore, Valerian
Helplessness	Bell Heather, Daisy, Grass of Parnassus, Monkey Flower
Home, feeling at	Balsam, Silverweed
Higher Self	Apple, Birch, Iona Pennywort, Mallow, Monkey Flower Rose Alba, Clear Light, Revelation
Higher Will	Apple, Mallow, Rose Alba
Honesty	Iona Pennywort, Scots Pine
Hope	Gorse, Rose Alba, Snowdrop
Hostility	Lime, Rowan, Willowherb, Karma Clear
Humanitarian	Globe-Thistle, Lime
Humility	Apple, Globe-Thistle, Grass of Parnassus, Iona Pennywort, Lime, Rowan, Silverweed, Willowherb
Hurt	Grass of Parnassus, Rowan, Karma Clear
Hysteria	Daisy, Grass of Parnassus, Wild Pansy, Scottish Primrose, First Aid
Illumination	Birch, Broom, Iona Pennywort, Lady's-Mantle, Wild Pansy, Clear Light
Illusion	Birch, Broom, Iona Pennywort, Lady's-Mantle, Scots Pine
Imagination	Birch, Lady's-Mantle, Clear Light

Immaturity	Daisy, Grass of Parnassus, Silverweed
Immortality	Elder, Rose Alba, Snowdrop
Immunity	Elder, Gorse, Grass of Parnassus, Sycamore, Watercress, Life Force
Impeccability	Globe-Thistle, Grass of Parnassus, Iona Pennywort, Rose Alba
Impotence	Apple, Gorse, Hazel, Rose Alba, Thistle, Willowherb
Incarnation	Balsam, Scottish Primrose, Stonecrop
Indecision	Broom, Daisy, Scots Pine, Clear Light
Indifference	Daisy, Lady's-Mantle, Lime, Spotted Orchid, Wild Pansy
Individuality	Hazel, Monkey Flower, Rose Alba
Inertia	Apple, Hazel, Spotted Orchid, Stonecrop, Revelation
Inferiority	Bell Heather, Holy-Thorn, Lime, Monkey Flower
Inflexibility	Globe-Thistle, Rose Alba, Stonecrop
Inhibition	Balsam, Grass of Parnassus, Holy-Thorn
Insanity	Birch, Iona Pennywort, Lady's-Mantle
Injustice	Lime, Rose Alba, Rowan, Scottish Primrose, Karma Clear
Inner child	Balsam, Bell Heather, Daisy, Elder, Grass of Parnassus, Monkey Flower
Inner conflict	Iona Pennywort, Scots Pine, Scottish Primrose, Rowan, Karma Clear
Inner guidance	Monkey Flower, Scots Pine, Rose Alba, Clear Light
Inner listening	Lady's-Mantle, Scots Pine, Clear Light
Inner peace	Grass of Parnassus, Scottish Primrose, Clear Light
Innocence	Daisy, Grass of Parnassus, Silverweed, Valerian
Insecurity	Bell Heather, Daisy, Grass of Parnassus, Rose Alba Sea Rocket
Insensitivity	Balsam, Grass of Parnassus, Mallow, Rose Alba, Wild Pansy, Willowherb
Insight	Birch, Broom, Lady's-Mantle, Rose Alba, Scots Pine, Clear Light, Karma Clear
Inspiration	Birch, Broom, Clear Light, Revelation
Instinct	Lady's-Mantle, Silverweed
Integration	Broom, Lady's-Mantle, Spiritual Marriage, Holy Grail
Integrity	Grass of Parnassus, Mallow, Silverweed, Mallow
Intellect	Broom, Lady's-Mantle, Clear Light
Intention	Apple, Hazel, Monkey Flower, Rose Alba
Intimacy	Balsam, Gorse, Grass of Parnassus, Holy-Thorn, Spiritual Marriage
Intimidation	Iona Pennywort, Monkey Flower, Rose Alba, Willowherb
Intolerance	Lime, Mallow, Willowherb
Introspection	Birch, Lady's-Mantle, Lime, Mallow, Spotted Orchid
Introversion	Birch, Grass of Parnassus, Lady's-Mantle, Monkey Flower, Spotted Orchid, Valerian
Intuition	Birch, Broom, Lady's-Mantle, Mallow, Rose Alba, Scots Pine, Clear Light
Irresponsibility	Daisy, Grass of Parnassus, Lime, Rose Alba, Silverweed, Valerian
Irritability	Globe-Thistle, Monkey Flower, Willowherb

Isolation	Balsam, Holy-Thorn, Lime, Rose Water Lily, Stonecrop
Jealousy	Holy-Thorn, Rowan, Karma Clear
Joy	Gorse, Elder, Grass of Parnassus, Valerian
Judgement	Iona Pennywort, Lime, Rose Alba, Rowan, Lime, Karma Clear
Karma	Birch, Iona Pennywort, Rowan, Karma Clear
Knowledge	Birch, Broom, Lady's-Mantle, Scots Pine
Kundalini	Apple, Sea Pink, Wild Pansy
Lack	Harebell, Sea Rocket
Laughter	Gorse, Valerian
Leadership	Apple, Laurel, Rose Alba
Learning	Broom, Lady's-Mantle, Scots Pine, Clear Light
Lethargy	Apple, Elder, Gorse, Hazel, Sycamore, Sea Pink, Wild Pansy, Life Force
Letting go	Hazel, Rowan, Stonecrop, Revelation
Liberation	Hazel, Globe-Thistle, Rose Water Lily, Snowdrop, Karma Clear, Revelation
Libido, increase	Balsam, Gorse, Holy-Thorn, Rose Alba
Life force	Elder, Gorse, Grass of Parnassus, Sea Pink, Sycamore, Wild Pansy, Life Force
Life purpose	Apple, Hazel, Revelation
Light	Birch, Gorse, Grass of Parnassus, Iona Pennywort Rose Water Lily, Wild Pansy, Clear Light
Lightness	Daisy, Elder, Snowdrop, Valerian, Revelation
Limitations	Birch, Hazel, Lady's-Mantle, Stonecrop, Revelation
Listening	Lady's-Mantle, Scots Pine, Clear Light
Loneliness	Balsam, Grass of Parnassus, Holy-Thorn, Lime, Stonecrop
Longevity	Elder, Gorse, Sycamore
Loss	Globe-Thistle, Hazel, Rose Water Lily, Snowdrop, Karma Clear
Love	Balsam, Holy-Grail, Grass of Parnassus, Mallow, Scottish Primrose
Lower self	Apple, Sea Pink, Silverweed, Willowherb
Lunacy	Birch, Daisy, Grass of Parnassus, Iona Pennywort, Lady's-Mantle, Sea Pink
Lust	Apple, Balsam, Grass of Parnassus, Iona Pennywort
Male/female balance	Grass of Parnassus, Mallow, Spiritual Marriage
Mania	Bell Heather, Daisy, Iona Pennywort, Scottish Primrose, Wild Pansy, Thistle, First Aid
Manifestation	Harebell, Laurel, Sea Rocket
Manipulation	Iona Pennywort, Rose Alba, Willowherb
Marriage	Balsam, Mallow, Sea Pink, Spiritual Marriage
Martyr	Globe-Thistle, Lime, Monkey Flower, Rowan, Valerian
Masculine	Rose Alba
Materiality	Harebell, Laurel, Sea Rocket, Silverweed, Watercress
Meditation	Broom, Lady's-Mantle, Scots Pine, Wild Pansy, Clear Light
Melancholy	Grass of Parnassus, Rowan, Spotted Orchid, Valerian
Memory	Broom, Lady's-Mantle, Wild Pansy, Clear Light
Menopause	Elder, Holy-Thorn, Sea Rocket, Stonecrop
Mental clarity	Birch, Broom, Lady's-Mantle, Wild Pansy, Clear Light

Miasms	Rowan, Watercress, Karma Clear
Mind	Birch, Broom, Lady's-Mantle, Mallow, Rose Alba, Wild Pansy, Clear Light
Mindfulness	Birch, Lady's-Mantle, Wild Pansy, Clear Light
Mistrust	Bell Heather, Holy-Thorn, Iona Pennywort, Lime
Moderation	Apple, Globe-Thistle, Sea Rocket, Silverweed, Watercress
Molestation	Balsam, Daisy, Holy-Thorn, Iona Pennywort, Rowan, Scottish Primrose
Money	Harebell, Laurel, Sea Rocket
Mood swings	Bell Heather, Daisy, Grass of Parnassus, Sea Rocket, Wild Pansy
Morality	Balsam, Grass of Parnassus
Mother	Balsam, Holy-Grail, Grass of Parnassus
Motivation	Apple, Gorse, Hazel, Monkey Flower, Rose Alba
Mourning	Grass of Parnassus, Hazel, Rowan, Snowdrop, Revelation
Narrow-mindedness	Birch, Lime, Lady's-Mantle, Silverweed, Spotted Orchid
Nature, attunement	Balsam, Silverweed
Negativity	Iona Pennywort, Rowan, Snowdrop, Spotted Orchid
Nervousness	Bell Heather, Daisy, Grass of Parnassus, Monkey Flower, Scottish Primrose, Sycamore, Valerian, Wild Pansy, First Aid
Nightmares	Iona Pennywort, Lady's Mantle, Snowdrop
Non-attachment	Apple, Globe-Thistle, Hazel, Snowdrop, Revelation
Nostalgia	Hazel, Spotted Orchid
Nurturing	Balsam, Elder, Holy-Thorn, Sea Rocket
Observer	Birch, Iona Pennywort, Lady's-Mantle
Obsession	Birch, Daisy, Grass of Parnassus, Iona Pennywort, Monkey Flower, Thistle
Obstinacy	Lime, Rose Alba, Rowan, Spotted Orchid, Stonecrop, Willowherb
Openness	Balsam, Grass of Parnassus, Holy-Thorn, Scots Pine Sea Rocket, Sycamore, Wild Pansy
Oppression	Iona Pennywort, Lime, Rose Alba, Willowherb
Optimism	Hazel, Snowdrop, Spotted Orchid, Sycamore, Valerian
Out of body	Balsam, Bell Heather, Birch, Lady's-Mantle, Scottish Primrose
Over-sensitivity	Daisy, Grass of Parnassus, Monkey Flower, Scottish Primrose
Overbearing	Rose Alba, Willowherb
Over-concern for others	Birch, Globe-Thistle, Scottish Primrose, Valerian
Overindulgence	Apple, Globe-Thistle, Silverweed, Watercress
Overwhelm	Daisy, Lady's-Mantle, Lime, Sea Pink
Overwork	Globe-Thistle, Sea Pink, Silverweed, Sycamore, Valerian
Pain	Grass of Parnassus, Rowan, Scottish Primrose, First Aid, Karma Clear
Panic	Grass of Parnassus, Rowan, Scottish Primrose, Snowdrop, First Aid, Karma Clear
Paranoia	Birch, Daisy, Iona Pennywort
Parenting	Balsam, Daisy, Holy-Thorn, Monkey Flower, Rose Alba
Passion	Balsam, Gorse, Grass of Parnassus, Rose Alba, Valerian
Past	Birch, Hazel, Rowan, Spotted Orchid, Stonecrop Patience Globe-Thistle, Hazel, Rose Alba, Stonecrop, Sycamore, Valerian

Peace	Grass of Parnassus, Globe-Thistle, Lime, Scottish Primrose Valerian, Watercress	115
Perception	Birch, Lady's-Mantle, Clear Light	
Perfection	Spotted Orchid, Holy Grail	
Perseverance	Apple, Hazel, Laurel, Monkey Flower, Rose Alba	
Personal relationships	Balsam, Holy-Thorn, Spiritual Marriage	
Pessimism	Hazel, Iona Pennywort, Spotted Orchid	
Pining	Balsam, Globe-Thistle, Hazel, Revelation	
Planetary consciousness	Exaltation, Globe-Thistle, Lime, Rose Alba	
Playfulness	Daisy, Gorse, Valerian	
Polarities	Iona Pennywort, Mallow, Sea Pink, Spiritual Marriage	
Positivity	Rose Alba, Spotted Orchid	
Possession	Daisy, Iona Pennywort, Scottish Primrose, Thistle	
Possessiveness	Harebell, Hazel, Holy-Thorn, Iona Pennywort, Mallow Sea Rocket	
Poverty	Harebell, Sea Rocket	
Power	Apple, Grass of Parnassus, Lime, Monkey Flower, Rose Alba Thistle, Willowherb	
Prejudice	Holy-Thorn, Lime, Rose Alba, Rowan	
Pride	Elder, Iona Pennywort, Lime, Rose Alba	
Procrastination	Apple, Laurel, Hazel, Stonecrop	
Promiscuity	Apple, Balsam, Iona Pennywort, Rowan	
Protection	Daisy, Iona Pennywort, Rose Alba, Watercress, First Aid	
Prudishness	Balsam, Grass of Parnassus	
Puberty	Daisy, Elder, Grass of Parnassus, Mallow, Monkey Flower	
Public speaking	Broom, Holy-Thorn, Lady's Mantle, Monkey Flower, Rose Alba Scots Pine, Clear Light	
Purification	Ragged Robin, Watercress, Wild Pansy	
Purity	Grass of Parnassus, Iona Pennywort, Ragged Robin Rose Water Lily, Sea Rocket, Watercress	
Purpose	Apple, Bell Heather, Daisy, Hazel, Monkey Flower, Rose Alba Clear Light	
Radiance	Globe-Thistle, Snowdrop, Wild Pansy	
Rage	Iona Pennywort, Monkey Flower, Wild Pansy, Willowherb	
Rebelliousness	Daisy, Lime, Rose Alba, Willowherb	
Receptivity	Grass of Parnassus, Lady's-Mantle, Mallow, Sea Pink Sycamore, Wild Pansy, Clear Light	
Reconciliation	Holy-Thorn, Lady's-Mantle, Lime, Mallow, Rowan, Karma Clear, Spiritual Marriage	
Recovery	Elder, Gorse, Globe-Thistle, Sea Pink, Sea Rocket, Sycamore, Watercress, Life Force	
Regression	Birch, Rowan, Karma Clear	
Rejection	Balsam, Holy-Thorn	
Rejuvenation	Elder, Gorse, Sea Rocket, Sycamore, Wild Pansy, Life Force	
Relationships	Balsam, Gorse, Lime, Mallow, Scottish Primrose, Sea Pink Spiritual Marriage	
Relaxation	Balsam, Hazel, Scottish Primrose, Sycamore, Valerian	

Release	Hazel, Rowan, Snowdrop, Stonecrop, Karma Clear, Revelation
Remorse	Globe-Thistle, Grass of Parnassus, Iona Pennywort, Rowan, Karma Clear
Renewal	Elder, Gorse, Iona Pennywort, Snowdrop, Sycamore, Watercress, Life Force
Repression	Balsam, Grass of Parnassus, Holy-Thorn, Iona Pennywort Monkey Flower, Rowan
Resentment	Grass of Parnassus, Globe-Thistle, Rowan, Karma Clear
Resignation	Apple, Globe-Thistle, Hazel, Monkey Flower, Rose Water Lily, Snowdrop, Sycamore
Resistance	Rose Alba, Stonecrop, Karma Clear, Revelation
Resourceful	Harebell, Laurel, Monkey Flower, Sea Rocket
Responsibility	Apple, Globe-Thistle, Laurel, Lime, Rose Alba, Valerian
Restlessness	Daisy, Hazel, Valerian, Wild Pansy
Restriction	Hazel, Scottish Primrose, Stonecrop, Wild Pansy
Resurrection	Rose Water Lily, Snowdrop, Revelation
Revelation	Lady's-Mantle, Stonecrop, Revelation
Revenge	Iona Pennywort, Lime, Rowan, Karma Clear
Rigidity	Globe-Thistle, Hazel, Lime, Rose Alba, Rowan, Stonecrop
Ruthlessness	Iona Pennywort, Rose Alba, Rowan, Willowherb
Sacrifice	Apple, Globe-Thistle
Sadness	Gorse, Grass of Parnassus, Rowan, Snowdrop, Valerian
Sarcasm	Lime, Rose Alba, Spotted Orchid, Willowherb
Scepticism	Lady's-Mantle, Lime, Scottish Primrose, Silverweed
Security	Globe-Thistle, Harebell, Hazel, Sea Rocket, Silverweed
Self-acceptance	Balsam, Elder, Holy-Thorn, Iona Pennywort, Monkey Flower
Self-aggrandisement	Rose Alba, Willowherb
Self-assertiveness	Apple, Monkey Flower, Rose Alba
Self-awareness	Iona Pennywort, Lady's-Mantle, Silverweed
Self-blame	Monkey Flower, Rose Alba, Rowan, Karma Clear
Self-centred	Lime, Silverweed, Spotted Orchid, Willowherb
Self-confidence	Bell Heather, Elder, Monkey Flower
Self-criticism	Balsam, Elder, Holy-Thorn, Monkey Flower
Self-deception	Iona Pennywort, Lady's-Mantle, Rowan, Scots Pine
Self-denial	Globe-Thistle, Valerian
Self-destruction	Globe-Thistle, Iona Pennywort, Rowan, Sea Pink, Watercress
Self-forgiveness	Birch, Grass of Parnassus, Rowan, Karma Clear
Self-empowerment	Monkey Flower, Thistle, Willowherb
Self-expression	Balsam, Broom, Grass of Parnassus, Holy-Thorn, Monkey Flower, Rose Alba, Spotted Orchid
Self-love	Balsam, Grass of Parnassus, Holy-Thorn
Self-neglect	Balsam, Globe-Thistle, Valerian, Watercress
Self-nurturing	Balsam, Gorse, Sea Rocket, Valerian
Self-pity	Globe-Thistle, Rowan
Self-punishment	Iona Pennywort, Rowan
Self-realisation	Hazel, Monkey Flower, Silverweed
Self-sabotage	Iona Pennywort, Globe-Thistle, Spotted Orchid

Self-worth	Bell Heather, Elder, Monkey Flower
Selfishness	Globe-Thistle, Silverweed, Willowherb
Senility	Birch, Daisy, Grass of Parnassus, Lady's-Mantle, Wild Pansy
Sensitivity	Balsam, Daisy, Grass of Parnassus, Lady's-Mantle, Valerian, Wild Pansy
Sensuality	Balsam, Elder, Gorse, Grass of Parnassus, Holy-Thorn, Sycamore
Separation	Balsam, Mallow, Snowdrop, Stonecrop, Revelation, Spiritual Marriage
Separativeness	Balsam, Lime, Rose Water Lily, Sea Pink, Stonecrop
Serenity	Grass of Parnassus, Scottish Primrose
Seriousness	Daisy, Globe-Thistle, Valerian
Service	Apple, Globe-Thistle, Laurel, Lime, Rose Alba
Sex	Apple, Balsam, Holy-Thorn, Rose Alba, Sea Pink
Sexual-abuse	Apple, Daisy, Globe-Thistle, Holy-Thorn, Rowan, Sea Pink, First Aid, Karma Clear
Sexuality	Apple, Balsam, Holy-Thorn, Rose Alba, Spiritual Marriage
Shadow self	Lady's-Mantle, Iona Pennywort
Shame	Balsam, Iona Pennywort, Rowan
Shock	Bell Heather, Daisy, Scottish Primrose, Thistle, First Aid
Shyness	Daisy, Elder, Grass of Parnassus, Monkey Flower
Simplicity	Daisy, Silverweed, Valerian
Sleep	Lady's-Mantle, Scottish Primrose, First Aid
Sluggishness	Elder, Gorse, Grass of Parnassus, Sea Pink, Stonecrop, Sycamore, Valerian, Life Force
Softness	Grass of Parnassus, Holy-Thorn, Sycamore
Soothing	Grass of Parnassus, Scottish Primrose, Sycamore, First Aid
Sorrow	Grass of Parnassus, Rowan, Karma Clear
Speaking	Mallow, Rose Alba
Spirit	Rose Water Lily, Clear Light, Holy Grail
Spontaneity	Gorse, Valerian
Stability	Bell Heather, Globe-Thistle, Sea Pink, Wild Pansy, First Aid, Spiritual Marriage
Strength	Bell Heather, Globe-Thistle, Iona Pennywort, Monkey Flower, Sycamore, Thistle, Watercress, Life Force
Stress	Bell Heather, Elder, Sycamore, Valerian, First Aid
Stubbornness	Rose Alba, Rowan, Silverweed, Stonecrop
Stuck	Hazel, Sea Pink, Spotted Orchid, Stonecrop, Revelation
Study	Birch, Broom, Daisy, Lady's-Mantle, Scots Pine, Clear Light
Subjugation	Apple, Globe-Thistle, Iona Pennywort, Sea Pink, Willowherb
Substance abuse	Apple, Globe-Thistle, Hazel, Iona Pennywort, Sea Pink, Snowdrop, Ragged Robin, Watercress
Suffering	Globe-Thistle, Scottish Primrose, Snowdrop, Rose Water Lily, Rowan, First Aid, Karma Clear
Suicidal	Holy-Thorn, Scottish Primrose, Snowdrop, Thistle, First Aid
Surrender	Globe-Thistle, Hazel, Rose Water Lily, Sea Pink, Snowdrop, Revelation
Survival	Sea Rocket, Silverweed, Thistle

Superiority	Apple, Lime, Rose Alba, Willowherb
Suspicion	Iona Pennywort, Lime, Rowan
Synergy	Lime, Lady's-Mantle, Mallow, Sea Pink, Wild Pansy, Holy Grail
Synthesis	Laurel, Lime, Sea Pink, Holy Grail, Spiritual Marriage
Tears	Grass of Parnassus, Rowan, Karma Clear
Teaching	Broom, Lady's-Mantle, Laurel, Rose Alba, Scots Pine, Clear Light
Telepathy	Birch, Grass of Parnassus, Lady's-Mantle, Scots Pine, Wild Pansy, Clear Light
Temper	Apple, Monkey Flower, Willowherb
Temperance	Apple, Iona Pennywort, Globe-Thistle, Sea Pink, Watercress, Willowherb
Tenderness	Balsam, Gorse, Grass of Parnassus, Holy-Thorn, Sycamore
Tension	Scottish Primrose, Sycamore, Rowan, Valerian, Wild Pansy, First Aid
Terror	Iona Pennywort, Scottish Primrose, Thistle, First Aid
Thinking	Broom, Hazel, Lady's-Mantle, Mallow, Wild Pansy
Thought patterns	Birch, Hazel, Lady's-Mantle, Iona Pennywort
Tiredness	Elder, Gorse, Sycamore, Valerian, Life Force
Timidity	Daisy, Elder, Grass of Parnassus, Monkey Flower
Tolerance	Globe-Thistle, Lime, Mallow, Rose Alba, Rowan, Spotted Orchid, Willowherb
Torment	Iona Pennywort, Rose Alba, Rowan, Thistle, Willowherb
Toxicity	Ragged Robin, Watercress
Transcendence	Rose Water Lily, Snowdrop, Stonecrop, Clear Light
Transformation	Grass of Parnassus, Snowdrop, Stonecrop, Watercress, Revelation
Transition	Hazel, Snowdrop, Stonecrop, Revelation
Tranquillity	Grass of Parnassus, Scottish Primrose, Watercress
Trance	Daisy, Iona Pennywort, Lady's-Mantle, Wild Pansy
Trauma	Bell Heather, Daisy, Rowan, Scottish Primrose, Thistle, First Aid
Trials	Bell Heather, Daisy, Iona Pennywort, Rowan, Thistle
True to oneself	Iona Pennywort, Monkey Flower
Truth	Iona Pennywort, Rose Water Lily, Scots Pine
Trust	Bell Heather, Hazel, Lady's-Mantle
Understanding	Birch, Lady's-Mantle, Rose Alba, Rowan, Scots Pine, Karma Clear, Revelation
Unconditional love	Holy-Thorn, Lime, Rowan, Scottish Primrose
Unification	Lime, Lady's-Mantle, Mallow, Sea Pink, Spiritual Marriage
Unity	Lime, Sea Pink, Spiritual Marriage
Universal Love	Exaltation, Lime, Scottish Primrose
Universal Mind	Birch, Clear Light, Wesak Blessing
Uplifting	Elder, Gorse, Grass of Parnassus, Rowan, Sycamore, Valerian, Revelation
Unreliability	Bell Heather, Daisy, Globe-Thistle, Iona Pennywort, Silverweed
Uprootedness	Balsam, Bell Heather, Daisy, Harebell, Scottish Primrose, Silverweed, Stonecrop
Vacillation	Daisy, Hazel, Mallow, Scots Pine, Sea Pink, Wild Pansy
Verbal abuse	Rose Alba, Willowherb

Victim	Bell Heather, Globe-Thistle, Grass of Parnassus, Lime, Monkey Flower, Rowan, Sea Rocket
Violence	Iona Pennywort, Scottish Primrose, Thistle, Willowherb, First Aid
Vision	Birch, Lady's-Mantle, Laurel, Clear Light, Revelation
Vitality	Gorse, Elder, Grass of Parnassus, Sea Pink, Sycamore, Valerian, Wild Pansy, Life Force
Vibrations, clearing	Grass of Parnassus, Ragged Robin, Sea Pink, Wild Pansy
Vulnerability	Balsam, Daisy, Grass of Parnassus
Weakness	Apple, Bell Heather, Globe-Thistle, Grass of Parnassus Sea Rocket, Sycamore, Thistle, Watercress
Will	Apple, Mallow, Rose Alba, Willowherb
Will-to-be	Balsam, Sea Pink, Snowdrop, Thistle
Will-to-good	Apple, Globe-Thistle, Laurel, Lime, Rose Alba
Wisdom	Lady's-Mantle, Scots Pine, Wesak Blessing, Clear Light, Holy Grail
Withdrawal	Balsam, Gorse, Globe-Thistle, Grass of Parnassus, Rowan, Sea Pink, Sea Rocket, Sycamore, Stonecrop, Snowdrop, First Aid, Revelation
Withholding	Holy-Thorn, Gorse, Grass of Parnassus, Monkey Flower, Rose Alba
Wholeness	Globe-Thistle, Holy-Grail
Workaholism	Apple, Globe-Thistle, Hazel, Sycamore, Valerian
Worry	Birch, Scottish Primrose, Valerian
Worrying, continual	Bell Heather, Monkey Flower, Valerian
Worthiness	Balsam, Elder, Holy-Thorn, Monkey Flower
Wounds	Rowan, First Aid, Karma Clear
Writing	Broom, Holy-Thorn, Rose Alba, Spotted Orchid, Clear Light
Xenophobia	Iona Pennywort, Holy-Thorn, Lime, Scottish Primrose

List of Findhorn Flower Essences
worldwide suppliers

UK
Findhorn Flower Essences
The Wellspring
31 The Park
Findhorn Bay
Forres IV36 OTY
Tel 01309 690129   Fax 01309 691300

The Phoenix Apothecary
The Park
Findhorn Bay
Forres IV36 OTZ
Tel 01309 691044   Fax 01309 690933

International Flower Essence Repertoire
The Working Tree
Milland
Liphook GU30 7JS
Tel 01428 741672   Fax 01428 741679

Germany
LF Naturprodukte
Treenering 105
Postfach 22
24851 Eggebek
Tel 04609 1526   Fax 04609 1535

Switzerland
Chrüeter-Drogerie Egger
Unterstadt 28
8200 Schaffhausen
Tel 052 624 5030   Fax 052 624 6457

Italy
Natur SRL
Via Settembrini 1
20124 Milano
Tel 02 6693950 Fax 02 6700708

Norway
Spiren as
Postboks 2527
7701 Steinkjer
Tel 074 167960   Fax 074 167961

U.S.A.
Flower Vision Research
244 Madison Avenue Suite 6H
New York NY 10016-2812
Tel 212 949 1973   Fax 212 949 8513

Flower Essence Pharmacy
6600 North Highway 1
Little River CA 95456
Tel 707 937 0441 Fax 707 937 5059

Harmonic Balance
P.O. Box 36923
Grosse Pointe
Michigan MI 48236
Tel 313 821 3445   Fax 313 821 3886

Australia
Nature's Energy
115 Glebe Point Road
Glebe N.S.W. 2037
Tel 02 9960 8342   Fax 02 9660 5584

Japan
Heart Support System
801, Okusawa Centre Mansion, 3-47-8
Okusawa, Setagaya-Ku, Japan 158
Tel 03 54997697   Fax 03 54997699

Brazil
Saguaro Import
Rua Andrea Paulinetti
102 Brooklin, Sao Paulo SP 04707-050
Brazil
Tel 011 535 2386   Fax 011 535 3994

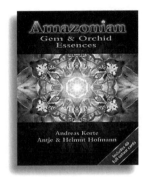

Nature Spirits & Elemental Beings

Marko Pogacnik

Although a lot has been written in recent years about nature spirits, this book by Slovenian author Marko Pogacnik is remarkable in that almost everything described in the book is based on his own practical experiences in communicating with these beings through meditation and tuning into plants, trees, animals and the landscape. He describes in detail the various elemental beings and their roles in maintaining the web of life, and also gives insights into related topics, such as the flow of energies within landscape, and the long-suppressed Goddess culture. His evocative images of the nature spirits draw our attention to the lost harmony of the natural world which has been disrupted by the impact of human culture.

£7.95/US$13.95 pbk 256 pages • ISBN 1 899171 66 5

The Golden Web

Gwennie Armstrong Fraser

The Golden Web is a symbol of the divine consciousness embracing Nature and humanity, infusing everything with its radiance and power. The divine Light glows at the centre of the web and radiates outwards, sustaining and illuminating all life. Each being and life form has a place within the interconnected whole. This book describes the urgent need for a new partnership with Nature through the messages from the Devic level of consciousness. The devas explain the levels of consciousness which we share with Nature and the profound beauty and light with which all life is created. They urge us to step forward together, deepen our connection with the natural world, and take active steps to begin the process of ecological restoration. In this book we can each discover our role.

£6.50/US$11.95 pbk 160 pages • ISBN 1 899171 25 8

Dialogue with Nature

Irene van Lippe Biesterfeld
(Princess Irene of the Netherlands)

People who talk to trees are often viewed with suspicion – even more so if they claim that the trees talk back to them and give them answers that help them in their daily lives!

Dialogue with Nature is therefore a unique testimony. Convinced that sharing her experience would be of help to so many of us who have lost our connection with nature, Irene van Lippe-Biesterfeld courageously offers an outstandingly intimate account of her relationship with the nature kingdom.

Throughout her childhood in the golden cages of royal palaces, and later her divorce and life as a single parent, Irene often felt misunderstood and even abandoned. At these times she turned to her friends in nature for refuge and solace, and there found peace and understanding.

£6.95/US$11.95 pbk 160 pages • ISBN 1 899171 86 X

Echoes of Camusfearna

Paul & Grace Yoxon

"Paul and Grace's touching and amusing stories of their life on Skye, and the founding of their wildlife rescue centre are set in the broader canvas of man's thoughtless and continuing destruction of nature and its wild animal inhabitants.

This book is for everyone – a sharing of experiences and feelings on a very personal level. It reveals a longing for the reader to "stand and stare", to be inspired by nature's wonders... and to protect them for future generations."

—Virginia McKenna
Star of "Ring of Bright Water" and "Born Free" and co-founder of the Born Free Foundation

£9.95/US$17.95 pbk 128 pages • ISBN 1 899171 76 2

The Findhorn Garden

The Findhorn Community

Beautifully illustrated, this book tells the story of the early days of the Findhorn Community and its communications with the nature intelligences or 'devas' underlying the physical forms of plants, trees and landscapes.

£9.95 pbk 196 pages • ISBN 0 905249 70 4

My Life My Trees

Richard St Barbe Baker

Conservationist, forester, founder of 'Men of the Trees', Richard St Barbe Baker was by any account a remarkable man. He worked with President Roosevelt to establish the Civil Conservation Corps, involving six million youths. More recently he started the 'Save the Redwoods' campaign in California and was instrumental in the planting of over 26 trillion trees internationally by organisations he founded or helped. This book tells his life story.

£5.95/US$10.95 pbk 168 pages • ISBN 0 905249 63 1

For a complete catalogue of Findhorn Press books and products, please fill in this form and send it to:

Findhorn Press
The Park
Findhorn
Forress
Moray
Scotland IV36 0TZ
fax +44 (0)1309 690036
email thierry@findhorn.org

Name _____

Address _____

_____

_____

Post Code/Zip _____

My special interests are _____

_____

_____

_____

_____

_____